The Anatomy of Fate

The Anatomy of Fate
Astrology and Kabbalah

Z'ev ben Shimon Halevi

Bet El Trust
Registered Charity No. 288712

www.ksbooksltd.com
E-mail: info@ksbooksltd.com

First published in 1978 by Rider & Co.
Revised Edition in 2009 by Kabbalah Society
Copyright © Z'ev ben Shimon Halevi 1978, 2009, 2024

Every effort has been made to obtain permission to reproduce copyright material but there may be cases where we have been unable to trace the copyright holder. The publisher will be happy to correct any omissions in future printings.

The moral right of the author has been asserted.

All rights reserved.
No part of this publication may be reproduced, stored in a retrieval system or transmitted, in any form or by any means, without the prior permission in writing of the publisher, nor be circulated in any form of binding or cover other than that in which it is published and without a similar condition including this condition being imposed on the subsequent purchaser.

A CIP catalogue record for this book
is available from the British Library.

ISBN 978-1-917606-20-2

Design by Lion Dickinson

For Solomon ibn Gabirol

By the same author:

Adam and the Kabbalistic Trees
A Kabbalistic Universe
The Way of Kabbalah
Introduction to the World of Kabbalah
Kabbalah and Exodus
The Kabbalist at Work
Kabbalah: School of the Soul
Psychology and Kabbalah
The Kabbalistic Tree of Life
Kabbalah and Astrology
The Anointed *A Kabbalistic Novel*
The Path of a Kabbalist
Kabbalistic Contemplations

By Other Publishers:

Kabbalah—The Divine Plan (HarperCollins)
Kabbalah, Tradition of Hidden Knowledge (Thames & Hudson)
Astrology, The Celestial Mirror (Thames & Hudson)
As Above So Below (Stuart & Watkins)

Contents

	Preface	xi
	Introduction	xiii
1.	Development of Knowledge	15
2.	Systems	23
3.	Macrocosm	31
4.	Body and Ascendant	41
5.	Planetary Body	47
6.	Mundane Astrology	54
7.	Descent into Flesh	64
8.	The Horoscope	70
9.	Planetary Emphasis of Psyche	79
10.	The Houses and the Ages of Man	88
11.	Unfolding Rhythms	99
12.	Prediction: A Sample Life	109
13.	Disease	117
14.	Moments of Crisis and Decision	127
15.	Degrees of Choice	136
16.	Sleeping and Awakening Suns	144
17.	The Psyche and its Contents	151
18.	The Soul	161
19.	The Spirit	169
20.	Evil, Free Will and the Cosmos	177
21.	Providence	186
22.	Death and Destiny	194

viii

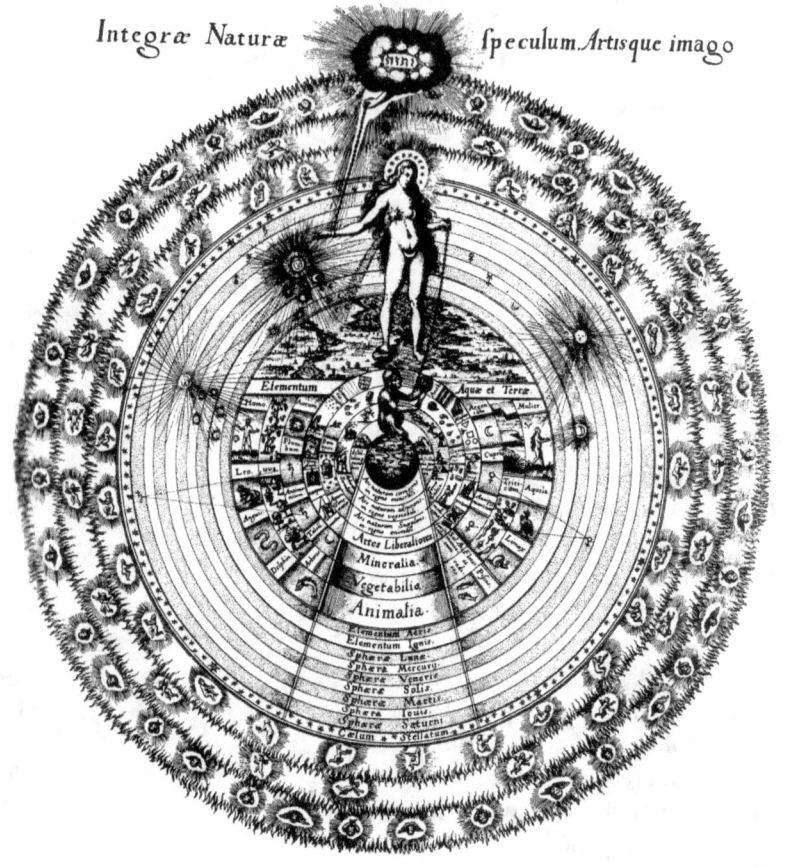

Figure 1—EXISTENCE
In this engraving, the Holy Name of YHVH is the source of the three higher Worlds of the Divine, the Spirit and the level of the soul. Within these spheres is the material universe, beginning with the stars, then the Solar system which encloses the Earthly realm. The female figure is a symbol of the Holy Spirit that pervades all the levels. Astrology is concerned primarily with life on Earth but its esoteric aspect leads to human development. (Robert Fludd, 17th century).

Illustrations

1.	Existence	viii
2.	Cosmic Clock	xii
3.	Astrology	16
4.	System	20
5.	Solar Orientation	26
6.	Kabbalistic Tree of Life	30
7.	Adam Kadmon	32
8.	Four Worlds	34
9.	Astral Realm	36
10.	Interaction	38
11.	Macro- and Microcosms	44
12.	Symbolism	50
13.	Earth and the Heavens	58
14.	Horoscope of the USA	60
15.	Incarnation	66
16.	Horoscope	73
17.	Zodiac	74
18.	Basic Psyche	78
19.	Tree Chart	82
20.	Triads	84
21.	Houses	89
22.	Ages	92
23.	Levels	95
24.	Wheel of Fortune	98
25.	Transits	105
26.	Progression	108
27.	Affliction	116
28.	Healing	120
29.	Confrontation	126
30.	Saturn Return	129
31.	Psychology	131
32.	Choice	137
33.	Decision	145

34.	Contents of the Mind	152
35.	Method	160
36.	Expansion	166
37.	Options	170
38.	Ascent	172
39.	Opposition	179
40.	Free Will	182
41.	Providence	187
42.	Death	196
43.	Evolution	201

Preface

Every life has an individual pattern. Some lives are full of incident and some are quiet, while others seem graced by good fortune or cursed by ill luck. Why is this? And what, many ask, is it that predetermines the flow of events and precipitates the crises that occur in our paths through life? Astrologers often describe in great detail the effects of this or that celestial configuration but rarely define the causes or the mechanics of how they actually influence us. The answers are to be found in the ancient Teachings behind astrology which add the spiritual dimension and indicate the Divine purpose to the anatomy of fate.

London, Autumn 1977

Figure 2 — COSMIC CLOCK
This mandala contains most of the principles and laws of astrology. The outer ring defines the Zodiac and the Mundane Houses. Within this comes the Sun, Moon and planets and the four elemental triangles of Earth, Water, Air and Fire along with their relation to the heavenly bodies and the signs. The innermost circles set out the classical gods and the physical manifestation of the Solar system which is but a material image of Divine processes. (Design by Halevi).

Introduction

Even before records were ever made, it is apparent that early mankind was aware of the influence of the Heavens. Many of the first monuments were alignments of stones that marked the rhythms of the Sun, Moon and the constellations. This appreciation of the celestial motions in relation to the seasonal round, methodically studied over many generations, became an important body of knowledge in nearly every evolving culture; so that, by the time the first full civilisation flowered, astrology was a recognised institution.

Perhaps the greatest discovery of the early period of collating celestial patterns was the observation of the positions of the planets and their correspondence with distinct terrestrial events in the history of peoples and in the lives of individuals. The detection of these subtle interplays brought about recognition of different qualities of celestial influence. From this discovery came the construction of a model of a multi-levelled Universe. At its centre is the Earth, the elemental and natural composition of which was clearly subject to the fluctuations of the surrounding macrocosm as it moved through a cosmic progression towards the end of Time.

From the above scheme of the Universe rose the inevitable question as to how, exactly, did human beings respond to this cosmic weather. Man, it was conceived, was the Universe in miniature and, as a microcosmic organism, resonated in sympathy to the macrocosm. This concept, and the way in which the processes of celestial influence operate, is examined in the work that follows. So too is the nature of fate, free will and the purpose of destiny for each of us who are incarnate for so brief a time between birth and death.

1. Development of Knowledge

The first premise that must be accepted as a point of departure is that there exists an objective reality. Such a reality will contain everything, including both the perfect and the imperfect, the true and the false. This objective Universe, moreover, can only be seen in its totality by the absolute eye of God. Anything less is subjective.

Any being within the Universe will perceive it with a greater or lesser degree of objectivity. This hierarchy of perception ranges from the lowest level of dense materiality, up through the metallic and mineral realms and the vegetable and animal kingdoms to man who occupies a position roughly half-way between the dimmest spark embedded in solid matter and the brilliant light of the Divine. The upper Worlds constitute increasingly greater degrees of consciousness, passing up through the cosmic realms to that level of perception and being which is just before union with the Godhead. Man, holding the midway position, is in a unique situation because he links the upper and lower Worlds. However, before we can examine the implications in this particular astrologically-angled study, we must begin at the beginning and see how the human intelligence began to perceive the world.

Early man was a creature of the senses; he found himself born into a physical situation where his psychological and spiritual faculties were either undeveloped or redundant. This was because, at the time of his arrival on the Earth, he had to cope with an organic body and survive in a tough natural and elemental habitat. At this stage of evolution he was little more than an animal himself, having evolved—or descended, according to one's beliefs—into a rather slight mammalian primate.

Taking the elemental level of perception of the outer world first, primitive man had to relate to a physical situation. This could be desert, grassland, forest or tundra. In these places he not only had to find a comfortable and safe site in which to live but also make allowance for the alternating heat and cold of day and night and Summer and Winter. Adjustment to the elements was a matter of life

Figure 3—ASTROLOGY
The study of the Heavens and their effect on the Earth and human affairs is ancient. Over millennia, observations of terrestrial and celestial cycles, and their different manifestations when combined, have built up a picture of distinct order. The rhythm of the ocean's tides, seasons and twelve types of human nature all indicated an integrated system within which a process of evolution was occurring, especially as regards history and individuals. These studies and conclusions formed the basis of astrology. (Medieval woodcut).

and death. Five senses gave him a very physical picture of the world about him.

The next level of his awareness was the vegetable part of his incarnate nature. His body, like all plants, needed an earth-based home for a root, even if it was just a cave, water to drink, air to breathe and light by which to be energised. Thus the vegetable aspect of him was sustained by the four elements. This also meant that he was under two sets of laws: the elemental, that confined him to a particular range of physical possibilities, and the vegetable that held him within a strict daily rhythm of waking, sleeping, eating, excreting and a lifespan of being born, maturing, propagating and dying. All these factors dominated his life and formed the basis of his world picture.

Over and above the fundamental survival problem came the animal part of his constitution. This differed radically from the elemental and vegetable levels because it had a subtler level of perception. The animal intelligence is essentially social. It relates first to its parent or group and possesses the recognition of association. However, perhaps the greatest difference between the animal and the two lower kingdoms is the factor of mobility. With this asset the creature can add a dimension to its location. While plants can turn towards water, air or light they are essentially static, whereas the animal is not and so the range of its moving perception of the world is totally different. Early man not only possessed this mobile dimension but yet another one because he, alone of earthbound creatures, could consider things in the abstract.

Thus it was that, while man was physically governed by elemental and natural laws, he could also rise above them. This was possible because he had the ability to view himself observing. Now, although it is known that animals dream, it is not apparent that they can think outside their inherent instinctive patterns. Moreover, they do not have the ability to adapt or learn as quickly and as deeply as man and so they are still more or less under the laws of the elemental and organic earth. Man, on the other hand, evolved out of the moment by moment sensual-bound condition into the possibility of considering what happened in the past and what might occur in the future. This is borne out by the presence, even among the most primitive of tribes, of stories about long-gone events and divination about what is to come. This faculty for conscious projection forward or backwards into time is unknown in the other organic kingdoms that only live day by day. Such an appreciation of the not *'here and now'* generated a unique perception of a non-physical world.

From this point of departure from the sensual dimension came the belief that behind every elemental phenomenon and vegetable and animal species lay an unseen intelligence; that indeed there was a supernatural World above the natural. This gave rise (and it occurred all round the globe) to a whole hierarchy of spirit beings who governed the various manifestations of the Universe. Out of this developed mythologies that mixed the history of the people with the actions of the gods. This appreciation of the Universe was not sensual but emotional. The form was expressed in sagas that described a world governed by fear, love, bravery, cowardice, grief, sacrifice and exaltation. Thus each culture developed the archetypal symbols of the terrestrial and celestial powers that surrounded mankind.

First there were the primal divinities of the earth and sky, then the lesser gods of the elements, animals and plants. This pantheon was slowly filled out by individual gods of particular rivers or mountains and later, as the heavens were seen to be more than a backdrop to the Sun and Moon deities, the constellations and the planets were enclothed in a very special variety of mythology.

The sky had this particular treatment because, of all the factors in the Universe, it was the least comprehensible. To begin with, it was the most remote thing in the environment and held a mystery far beyond the most inaccessible earthly seashore or mountain range. Nothing but the luminaries, the planets, the stars and the Milky Way lived in the vast cosmic cave that over-shadowed the Earth. No birds, not even the great eagle, could stay up for as long as the Sun. Here was a strange world inhabited by many elemental moods, sometimes calm, at others violent, and behind these windy and watery states there was the ever-moving changes of light and darkness. During the Summer days, the Solar disc was all powerful above the Earth, although at night he gave way to his gentler consort the Moon who, as his feminine counterpart, had her waxing and waning temperament like the female of every species in the natural World below. These similitudes in the male and female combinations inevitably gave the Solar and Lunar archetypal symbols their particular character and so the coming together, perhaps in an eclipse, or the separation at night when the Moon was fully herself, bred many stories, cast in human form, about the relationship of the celestial husband and wife. The planets were likewise treated, each god and goddess's image generated by the peculiar brightness, colour and characteristic movement. All over the Earth remarkably similar archetypes were invented to describe, for example, Mars who was considered, by his red colour and sudden advances and retreats, to be warlike. In contrast Venus, with her clear blue sheen, was seen by many cultures to be feminine and beautiful; and Saturn, the slow, dim mover through the constellations, was inevitably felt to be like an old man, a watcher of events celestial and terrestrial.

So it came, in the passage of time as cultures blended into civilisations, that the poetic cosmic sagas also merged as the archetypes. Venus, for instance, called Aphrodite in Greece, Ishtar in Assyria, Astarte in Phoenicia and Nana in Babylon, slowly focused into a single image. All this was again set against the gradually refining symbolic picture of the constellations. Now, while many of the unsophisticated still saw the Milky Way, for example, as the road of the aristocratic dead and departed, the intelligent, with the aid of observation in conjunction with the already ancient records, began to perceive yet another dimension beyond the emotional picture of the Universe. This precipitated the intellectual appreciation of the order, number and logic of the Heavens.

The concept of order in Creation was a self-evident one, even to the mostly ignorant. Nature continually demonstrated it in the progress of the seasons and in the processes of birth, propagation and death. By the time that mankind had invented records and writing it was apparent that the sky rotated once a day in one direction and once a year in the other, as stars returned to an annual position. Besides the obvious use of this knowledge for calendars in which planting, river floods and festivals could be calculated to the day, the subtler rhythms of the planets were observed in the eases and tensions of particular times. This phenomenon was over and above the Solar phases of the year and the Lunar effects on terrestrial tides of water and growth of plants. This, in turn, made the thinkers perceive that there was a hierarchy of celestial influence, namely the Lunar, planetary, Solar, stellar and galactic levels of the Universe. Out of this came the system rooted in the original Sumerian cosmology, formalised about 3,000 BCE, in which the cupola of the sky contained the visible while, above, the gods ruled from the invisible realms beyond. Later, the dome was adapted as a base for celestial co-ordination in which the Heavens were divided into sectors with a grid relating to the Sun's ecliptic. Also added were the Northern- and Southernmost lines of the Sun's tropical positions. This format came to be known as the Celestial Sphere. The scheme was further calibrated by the Greeks according to the degrees or days of the year and their twelve Solar-Lunar divisions of the Zodiac.

Figure 4—SYSTEM
Over time, this first Theory of Relativity emerged. It was based upon the view from the Earth and what could be observed. Its concept primarily considered the influences that impinged upon the planet. These were seen in the plant and animal cycles as well as the rise and fall of cultures and civilisations which clearly—like individuals—had distinct astrological characters. Initially the Sun, Moon and planets were viewed as gods but Abraham, who lived in Ur of the Chaldees, the city of astrologers, believed there was an absolute Deity that governed all. Here began Kabbalistic astrology. (16th century woodcut).

DEVELOPMENT OF KNOWLEDGE

About this time, the evaluation of the planets in each sign and their active and passive rulership was resolved. So too was the sub-schema of the elemental and Cardinal, Mutable and Fixed factors in the Zodiac and the major angular relationships between the heavenly bodies. Enclosing this detailing was the rationalised model of Creation which attempted to explain, in a mixture of allegory and observational fact, the origin and structure of Existence. This now classical world picture has been preserved in the Ptolemaic formulation which describes one of the early theories of relativity in which the Earth pivots a geocentric set of spheres.

These were arranged in order of greater and lesser influence and not, as many later scientists thought, as a literal model of the Solar system. The ancient world used a blend of oriental art and occidental logic to define a Universe that could not just be perceived as a celestial machine.

Over what must have been, in relation to the many millennia of collecting data, a very short period of two hundred years, the system upon which astrology is based was designed. Where this actually occurred is not so important as the fact that at around the same period of 600 to 400 BCE the Chinese, the Greeks and the Jews, for example, were formulating their metaphysical systems. So it is of no surprise to discover in the Middle East that the preoccupation with celestial mechanics crystallised into a detailed teaching on the laws of the heavens and the effects of the luminaries and planets. This precipitated the first true horoscopes.

At this point the elemental, vegetable, animal as well as emotional and intellectual phases were brought together and fused into a system which, except for details and minor additions, has been with us for over two thousand years. Having reached its peak, astrology then entered a plateau of refinement in which the creative work of perhaps quite a small body of people became tradition. By this is meant that it was handed on in its crystallised form. While such a thing is excellent as long as there are people with a real grasp of the subject around to instruct, there automatically sets in the seeds of decay if there are not. This occurs because the passage of generations causes the vernacular of an earlier time either to become fixed as a sacred language or to be rejected as old-fashioned by later generations. Thus, if a tradition is not periodically reformulated it degenerates into teaching by rote, then learning from scriptures, and finally becomes no more than a fragmentary and often distorted version of the original system. There are many examples of this process, the most obvious one being the Tarot system which has become, for most, an instrument of superstitious consultation.

By Roman times, astrology had divided into three levels. The degenerate level was the garbled adulteration of fairground, market place and back street divination. Indeed, one emperor banned all astrologers from Rome (except his personal one) because they had such a noxious influence upon the citizens. This level is principally superstition and is practised by the charlatan or the person who believes without reason that he possesses knowledge. The phenomenon of ignorance awed by a little knowledge and some theatrical devices has occurred throughout the ages and has masked serious astrology with a dubious reputation. The two other classes of astrologers may be seen as the learnèd and the wise. The former make up the main body of practitioners. They are the people who, over the generations, continue the tradition and collect the highly valuable data that is used by the latter who speculate and deepen the Art-Science. This small body are those who see astrology as more than a system of individual or mundane analysis and prediction. They view astrology, as the original formulators did, as an esoteric Teaching on the Universe with all its laws embodied in the interconnection between the macrocosmic scheme of the world and the microcosmic image of man. This is the approach we shall attempt to explore.

2. Systems

Returning to the first premise that there is an objective Universe, wise men down the ages have tried to formulate an approximate picture of it by various means. In order to do this a series of stages have to be passed through before any readable image appears for anyone actually to perceive. The first stage is, of course, the realisation that there is an objective Existence, that what is perceived by the senses is in fact the resultant effect of many deep causes. This leads to the inquiry into the nature of these unseen causes and the further realisation that these causes are, again, effects governed by laws which themselves are based on first principles. These principles, that is the most basic set of causes in the Universe, are arrived at by a mixture of tradition and revelation.

Tradition is that which is handed down from one generation to another or from a teacher to a pupil. In most cases it is the knowledge that has been collected and verified over many centuries. This tends to give it a formal patterning, sometimes simple in presentation and sometimes elaborate in exposition, depending on the depth and weight of the knowledge and the way in which that tradition likes to preserve and teach its understanding. An example of this is the contrast between the long detailed conversations of Socrates and his disciples and the terse but loaded comments of some Zen masters. In essence, tradition is a gradual building up of a body of knowledge which is transmitted by study, discipline and contemplation. This is, for the most part, the history of astrology.

Revelation is of quite a different order. It is the revealing of knowledge by deep insight and the penetration of the veil of ignorance by a flash that connects things that seemed in no way related or did not have this or that implication. Here is the moment of discovery. As the word 'dis-covery' says, it is the uncovering of something already there, like a new country or law as yet unknown. The history of ideas is scattered with these rare incidents and though they occupy only a small space and time they nevertheless carry as much weight and depth as the laboriously put together conclusions of tradition. Thus it is that an

Einstein sitting before his fireplace, fixed in revelatory thought, can bring about the key to atomic energy; or the Buddha, seated under a tree, can see the way out of carnal suffering. Revelation in astrology is those moments of illumination which have fused the masses of data into rules, laws and principles upon which the system is based.

A system is a working body of knowledge. Theory on its own is only speculation. Without practice or function it has no real meaning or veracity. Thus, while there has long been an atomic theory there has only recently been a viable system of practical application based upon the theorem. Once the atom had been split and made to work to order, atomic physics became a system. From perceptive observation of life, history and everyday things, it is soon apparent that all working systems are based upon universal principles. Thus, for example, the body is a biological system with subsystems within it; so too is the organisation of nations which are based upon the government of tribes and the family unit. Even manufactured objects as simple as a child's scooter or as complex as a jet engine are based upon systems. Break one wheel or engine part and the machine or mechanical system ceases to work. From all this can be inferred that there is a set of interacting regulations which apply the laws that have been created by first principles. So it is that the first principle of the wheel runs through many machines. Sometimes, for example, the principle is set in the laws of the gear or the shaft, the turbine or the tyre. These in turn are governed by the regulators of numbers of teeth, speed or diameter and so on. All indicate a hierarchy of control and forces under direction. It is likewise with a system concerned with the principles, laws and regulations of the Universe.

The Universe is the primal example and model for every subsystem contained within it. Like its internal imitators, which only copy a particular functional aspect of its full capacity, the Universe is made up of rules, laws and principles. These, for most people, are way out of sight because they are either too large in scale or too minute to be noticed or because they are not connected with perceivable phenomena in the physical and psychological spectrum. Nevertheless, these principles exist and work through the natural world, governing and holding it together as moment-by-moment it exchanges energy with matter and back again. Because these levels of activity are not noticed, it does not mean that they are not there. The suspicion that there was more than could be sensually perceived began the first inquiry into the hidden nature of the world and its purpose.

SYSTEMS 25

Over the millennia of tradition and revelation the true structure and dynamics of the Universe unfolded themselves to the most evolved members of mankind. How to convey this knowledge to others outside the immediate study circle and to pass it on to future generations, so that they would not have to cover the same ground or repeat the same mistakes, was a problem. This precipated the necessity for an intelligible system. Based on experience and fact it has been concluded again and again, in different cultures and times in history, that the best way to transmit a body of knowledge about the Universe was to construct a symbolic model based upon the original: namely the principles, laws and regulations of Existence. This meant formulating a fundamental metaphysical scheme. Such a thing recurs all over the world, irrespective of time and place, and is quite recognisable by the discerning mind despite the overlay of culture or the distortion of the original presentation by decadence.

The most common example found in many cultures is the principle of the Trinity. This is seen in the three Hindu gods of Creation, Maintenance and Destruction, the yin-yang and neutral principles of Taoism, the three Divine attributes of Mercy, Grace and Justice in Judaism and the much misunderstood principle behind the Christian Trinity. These are, in fact, only fragments of a total scheme embodied in each religion. In the case of astrology there is a difference because astrology is closer to a teaching philosophy than a true religion. To be precise, astrology is an ancillary system of knowledge to several major systems. This is because it lacks a doctrine or personality (Divine or human) to make a formal religion. It does, however, still stand in its own right as a complete picture of the Universe and has thus survived most of the early religions which were its contemporaries in the ancient world. A complete system is one that points to the total picture of reality or at least takes into account all the factors in general if not in particular. Thus it is that while modern medicine may study, in the finest detail, fractions of the physical body and its workings, very little is taken into account of the psychological organism, not to mention the ailments of the spirit which may well be the generators of physical diseases. Modern medicine, for all its technology, is an incomplete system. When the states of the other two bodies of psyche and spirit are taken into consideration, then medicine can be called truly the science-art of healing.

A total system is one that includes the whole. By classical times most bodies of knowledge that had been formulated around the great

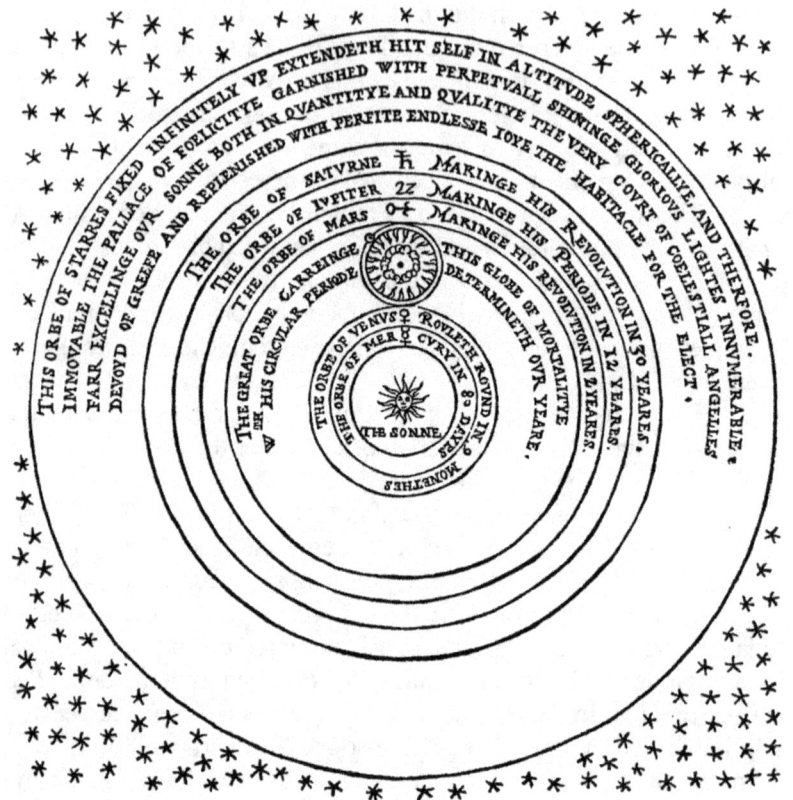

Figure 5—SOLAR ORIENTATION
With the advent of the telescope and science, the medieval view of an Earth-centred universe became redundant. The Sun was now the centre. Moreover, the symbolic understanding of celestial influences was dropped in favour of a purely physical model. This was ironic because Sir Isaac Newton, the formulator of celestial mechanics, was an astrologer. His retort to an astronomer who rubbished the ancient art was that it was clear the man either spoke from a thorough study of astrology or total ignorance. (Digges' woodcut of Solar system, 16th century).

creative period of 500 BCE were based upon a complete picture of the Universe. Nothing was seen as separate from everything else. The macrocosm was under the laws of the first Divine principles, while the microcosm was contained within the macrocosm which it reflected and followed in miniature at a lower level in Creation. Thus, for example, in China the Yin and Yang principles of opposites were seen in the big scale of good government and in the small scale of the human body; while in the Middle East the Jews based their secular customs upon the twin complements of duties and rights and their religion upon the dual approach of the love and fear of God. Everything in Existence, right down to the ordinary chores of life, was perceived as one interconnecting chain of smaller and larger links that became simpler, yet more potent as the level rose to a peak of Divine unity from which everything emanated.

This total view was carried by Western civilisation right through to the seventeenth century, when the advent of anthropocentric thought and the rise of physical science shattered the whole world picture and reduced Western man to the sensual and mechanical perception of reality. For instance, instruments like Galileo's telescope revealed to contemporary natural philosophers that the luminaries and the planets were not as they had been led to believe by the ancient teachers. The Sun's pure disc had blemishes, the Moon a rough mountainous face and some planets possessed satellites of their own, while Saturn had strange rings. With one glimpse through the telescope that every fashionable gentleman of the time had to procure, the whole allegorical aspect of the Universe evaporated. Suddenly, ordinary natural men of the Western world believed they could see with their sensual eye more of the Universe than the thinkers of ancient times and, therefore, all the ideas about the relationship of the various cosmoses were clearly redundant. Within two generations the complete world picture accepted by the Elizabethans had vanished and the very partial and entirely mechanical view, held up till quite recently, took its hold on the Western cultural establishment.

However all was not lost. While the 'Age of Reason,' as the new period came to be called, was examining the physical aspects of Creation through the bigger and better instruments, small groups of people dotted round Europe retained the total view in various occult and esoteric studies. These ranged from the scholarly groups hidden within the rapidly changing university situation to the secret societies of the Rosicrucians and the Masons. Within this spectrum, however, were the three sublevels of superstition, learning and wisdom. Some groups, for example, were indeed no more than cranks reacting blindly against the new mechanistic outlook while others diligently examined ancient Teachings without possessing the vital key of insight. Yet others knew something but became preoccupied with magical power and thus forgot the purpose of spiritual work. Fortunately, the level of wisdom was still to be found here and there and traces of it have been detected in England, Holland and Germany in the presence of men like Fludd, van Helmont and Boehme who saw the Universe as one unified organisation.

The situation today again has greatly changed. After several hundred years of the dominance of the partial science of natural philosophy, the West in particular has had to look again at the concept of the interconnection of everything. The reason for this is that by the end of the nineteenth century the mechanistic view had reached its limits. At the macrocosmic end of science, the great telescopes seemed to fall pathetically short of gaining a real grasp of the scale of Creation despite the vastly increased size of the lens, mirrors and light technology. Infinity could not be photographed or spectrographed. Moreover, a whole new radio Universe was later discovered which pushed back the scientific horizon and revealed a vast subtle complex of vibrating forces and radiant flows which had, until then, been unsuspected except by the ancients who had described it in allegory by such terms as 'the music of the spheres.' On the microcosmic front, the apparent solidity of matter had dissolved in laboratory experiments with the atom that uncovered a yet smaller entity which on alternate days could be thought of as a pulse of energy or a packet of matter. Einstein completed the overthrowing of the concept of the mechanical Universe by perceiving time in an entirely new way, so that common sense or sensual logic was no longer valid. All this, together with the rediscovery of our planet's magnetosphere and ecological system, made scientific inquiry begin seriously to consider that more lay beyond the scientifically observable processes and that, as ancient and occult teachings stated, perhaps even subtler forces existed beyond the Earth and deep within the human being.

Experiments that would have been considered professionally damaging at the beginning of the twentieth century have now become respectable and the general interest in the paranormal has increased the demand by many intelligent people to investigate and speculate, in a responsible manner, many of the phenomena regarded for three centuries as superstitious nonsense. This has created a situation in which those who have been seriously concerned with the perennial truth about the objective Universe are obliged to reformulate the original model to meet the needs of this time and culture.

The problem, as always, is to blend ancient and modern in such a way as to open the connection in the contemporary view, not only to present-day reality but also to the objective Existence that has, is and always will be here to the end of Time. Such a task is not easy, especially as in this current examination of astrology where so many preconceived notions—some too much for and some too much against—exist. The middle position is where I hope you, the reader, will make your stand. I, for my part, will state my own position so that you can take into account the flavour of my bias because we are all subjective in our views to a greater or lesser degree. My own approach to astrology is upon a kabbalistic base. Kabbalah is the ancient inner teaching system of Judaism. However, this simply means that it is one particular form of the perennial truth about God, the Universe and Man. It happens to be my cultural background. It is important to bear in mind that although I shall draw on what appear to be two distinctly different theoretical systems, plus practical examples I shall, in fact, be speaking always of the same objective reality.

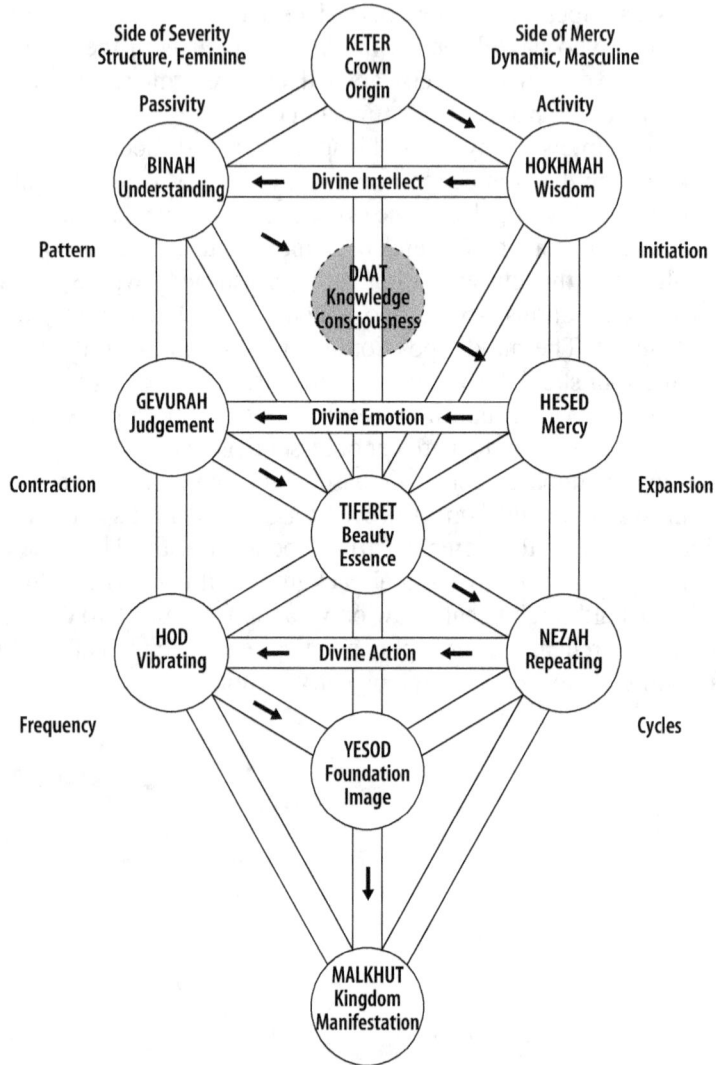

Figure 6 — KABBALISTIC TREE OF LIFE
This diagram contains the laws and principles that govern Existence. The arrows depict the Lightning Flash line of an octave while the three pillars indicate the principles of active, passive and neutral factors that operate within the levels and triads of the scheme. The paths relate to the twenty-two decorations of the menorah, the seven-branched candlestick in the Tabernacle of Moses with its two wings and three nodal points on the central column. This is, in essence, a metaphysical picture of the sefirot or ten Divine Numbers and the twenty-two letters of the Hebrew Alephbet. (Halevi).

3. Macrocosm

The exposition that follows is an unfolding of the background cosmology within which Astrology functions. Over the ages, people have used the three basic languages of mankind to elucidate the story of how Existence came into being. Some spoke in the terms of concrete action such as in buildings, the dance and ritual; others used allegory, explaining via the emotional tongue of myth and artistic imagery the emergence, bloom and return of Existence to its source; yet others described this process intellectually, setting out complex metaphysical schemes containing the delicate interplay of celestial intricacies as they work out the impulse that first put them in motion. We will use a blend of the emotional and intellectual approach, beginning with the most universal notion—that before the existence of anything there was *Nothing*.

It is said that God does not exist. That is to say that God is beyond Existence. That prior to Existence coming into being there was No-thing and that when God willed it, Existence emerged out of Nothing into Something. This One Thing or Oneness was to be the groundbed of everything that was to come into Existence. Should God's will cease, Existence would vanish and everything in it return to No-thing. However, Tradition tells us that it is God's purpose that Existence should not only emerge but develop so that God might behold God's reflection in the Mirror of Existence which is made in God's image.

The image of God is not God, although it might reflect all the Divine Attributes. So it came about, Tradition tells us, that the ten basic aspects of Divinity emanated out of No-thing into manifestation. It was, is and shall be for as long as Existence is willed to exist, the eternal and unchanging model upon which all other lesser manifestations are based. As the Divine image of God it acts as the intermediary between the Godhead and the lower Worlds that were to be created. This first manifestation of principles is the instrument of Divine Government through which God's will unfolds its purpose. Called by many names in different traditions it is known in the West as 'The

Figure 7 — ADAM KADMON
The Divine realm of the sefirot can also be seen as a humanoid figure composed of the Holy Name, YHVH, when written in Hebrew in a vertical mode. In Kabbalah, it is called the KAVOD or GLORY and represents the primordial World of Emanation, the closest dimension to the Absolute which is beyond Existence. The Zodiacal Man depicted in medieval manuscripts is an astrological version. It is from here that all human beings come, each one a cell of Divinity or spark of pure consciousness. This original Adam is also the place to which all will return at the End of Time. (Calligraphy by Halevi).

World without End' and the World of Azilut in Kabbalah. Azilut is a Hebrew word meaning both to 'emanate' and 'to stand near,' that is to emanate from and to stand near the Godhead.

In the Kabbalah there is a metaphysical diagram of this, the highest World. (There are many such schemes around the world but this is the one that is the most used in the West). In it the ten Divine attributes or principles are set out according to a definite arrangement. These principles give rise to universal laws and these laws give rise to minor rules and regulations because the hierarchy of sequence exists even in this most perfect of realms. Beginning at the top, from which the whole flows out, is what is called the Crown. This is the first principle, that is, All that come into Existence is rooted in the One Source. It is the place of equilibrium. On the right is the attribute or sefirah, as it is called, of Wisdom which represents the active aspect of Existence. Opposite is the sefirah of Understanding which makes up the passive aspect. These are the three primal laws or the classic Trinity that brings Existence into being, maintains it and dissolves it. The law of One is at the top and the law of opposites is embodied in the active Wisdom and passive Understanding and, together, they make the Trinity found in other Traditions. This supernal triad, along with the others that flow out of them, are the models that set the framework and dynamic that operate throughout the Universe.

The lower attributes are all subject to the first three principles and are arranged down the active, passive and neutral pillars of the Tree of Life, as the Kabbalistic diagram in Figure 6 is called.

The names are, at first, strange choices but in time they take on rich meaning for anyone who studies the Tree in depth. We are not going to penetrate, in this study, too deeply into the nature of the Tree but simply sketch out the general scheme so that we can see how the same principles apply in different Worlds and so perceive how the microcosm resonates with the macrocosm.* The rest of the Tree of Life is composed of a series of greater and lesser triads. Besides the topmost or Supernal Trinity, the greater are made up of the principles of Mercy, Judgement and Beauty, which occupy the middle zone, and the principles of Eternity, Reverberation and Foundation which form, with the Kingdom at the bottom, two lower triads. The relevance of the upper, middle and bottom levels will become apparent later in the construction of man who is based upon this same model. The lesser triads are those

---

*For a detailed account of the Tree of Life see the author's other books published by Kabbalah Society.

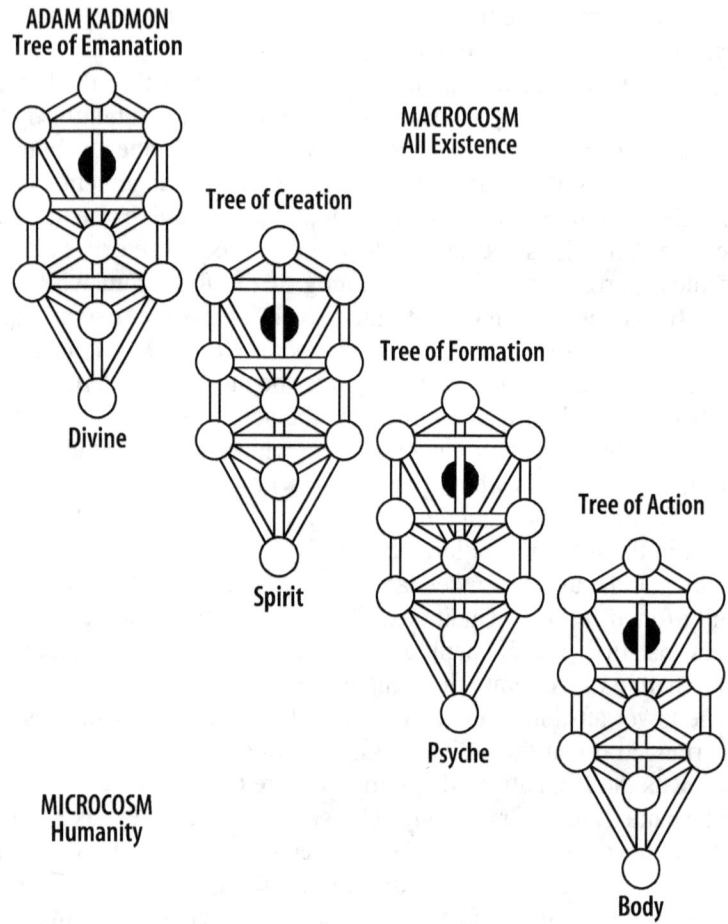

Figure 8—FOUR WORLDS
Based upon the design of the Tree of Emanation, three lower Worlds then emerge. The first is that of Creation, the realm of the Spirit. Then comes the World of Formation which corresponds to the domain of the soul or psyche. This is the dimension of astrology. Below is the material World of Nature and the four elements. It is here where human souls take on physical bodies at birth. This elemental vehicle, through Evolution, incorporates the mineral, vegetable and animal levels. While the four Worlds are separate, they do overlap and interconnect. (Halevi).

composed by the paths, as they are called, connecting the side sefirot (plural of sefirah). These define the functional aspects of Existence as against the consciousness of the central column triads. In analogy they are the unconscious intelligence of the arms and legs in contrast to the conscious awareness of the mind and heart of a person. Indeed, in early kabbalistic literature the symbol of a Great Man was used to explain the left and right side functions and the central will of Divinity. Out of this perfect image came the later and lesser image of the Celestial or Zodiacal man who is a mirror of his maker in a lower World.

The lower Worlds, we are told, were created out of the first Eternal one. As a perfect World there was no movement, therefore there was no development or space for action. It was a paradox. Besides, this Divine World was only one remove from the Godhead and so in the Will to behold Himself, Tradition tells us, God set in motion Creation, so that a greater distance might be made in which God could view the image of God more fully. Thus Creation emerged out of the perfect World of Divine Emanation. This was to be the second of four Worlds that had their origin in the four levels within the World without End.*

Creation is the beginning of time. It is the World that shifts Existence out of the perfect stillness of Eternity into the unfolding of the cosmic flower, as some traditions see it, which takes all of time to bloom and fade as billions of creatures pass through the cycle of the cosmic year. Creation is the World where things begin to become; that is, they emerge out of the movement of the Universe in the same way as Spring leaves emerge out of Winter trees. All things brought into being are miraculous events in Creation. They come about because the Will of the Divine, working through the principles or sefirot of Creation, brings an idea into manifestation. Thus all things and creatures move with the flow of time, each one having its season on a cosmic scale.

According to Kabbalah, the second World of Creation is the first level of separation. This is the first true remove from the direct contact with the Godhead. Here begins deviation, contrast, conflict and choice. But this, we are told, is Divine intention, because it makes for—as one Tradition puts it—a much more interesting cosmic game. This element of choice and hazard, and the temptation of evil, is also to test the good and strengthen the weak. How else can the good be

---
*For details see author's *A Kabbalistic Universe*, (Kabbalah Society)

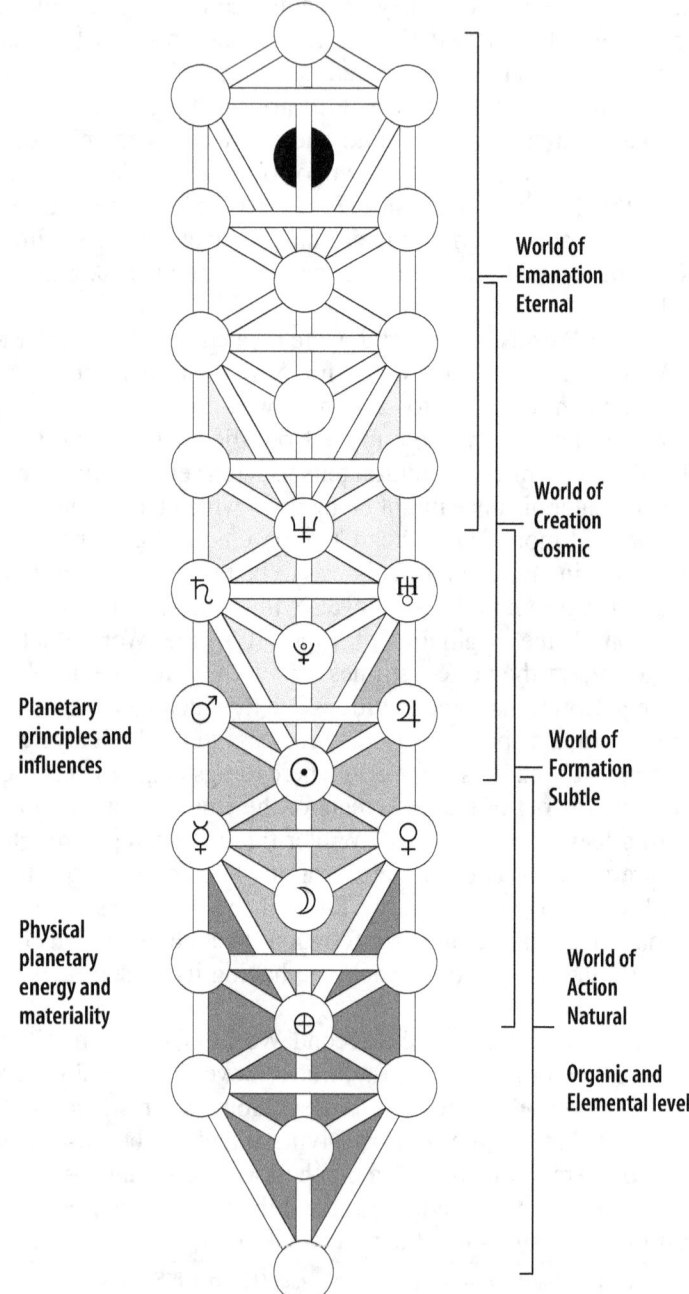

proved to be so and the weak grow? On the large cosmic scale of Creation, success or failure and life and death have quite a different meaning. There is always next season's set of games to be played and the time is as long as Creation exists to learn the arts of Existence. Another aspect of this second World is that it is penetrated by the first World, that is to say, like light permeates air, so Emanation or Divinity percolates the World of Creation. This means not only that the actual presence of the Divine is everywhere at all times but also that there are, at the creative level, two sets of laws to be obeyed, the Divine and the Cosmic. The implication is that the Universe, at this stage, has a more complex structure and this principle is repeated with each additional descending level. To illustrate such a point we can see how the first World is composed of principles and the second of laws. These laws are, in themselves, composed of principles which give rise to creative laws, rules and regulations. The result of this increased complexity is that there is less manoeuvrability. Thus, for example, there are two complementary factors now in existence; the active, expanding sefirot of Creation on one side and the passive, constraining sefirot of Creation on the other. This notion is expressed in the two outer pillars of the Tree of Creation which emerges out of the original Tree of Emanation which is behind the laws of Creation.

Out of the World of Creation emerges a third level of Existence. This is called the World of Formation in Kabbalah. It is known as the astral, planetary or subtle World in other Western Traditions. It is quite different from the other two upper Worlds in that it is said to be of a fluidic nature, that is, it shifts into and out of various forms. Its purpose is expressed in this watery quality inasmuch as its fluidity holds the ever-moving forms. Thus the beings of the created World can develop in a medium which is continually altering its form as the Universe passes through the descending and ascending phases of Creation and Evolution.

The World of Formation is called the planetary World because it is

---

Figure 9 (Left)—ASTRAL REALM
Here the four Worlds are aligned in what is called Jacob's Ladder. As such, their different influences flow up and down. In the case of the Solar system, the astral realm affects what occurs on Earth. The Sun, for example, has an eleven-year cycle which has an impact on human activity, creating fluctuations in politics and trade. Jupiter, in certain signs, stimulates growth in many fields while Saturn can slow progress. Each of the planets has a distinct quality according to its position in the Tree of Formation. The Moon, being the lowest celestial body, has the most obvious influence although this is too subtle for most people to detect. (Halevi).

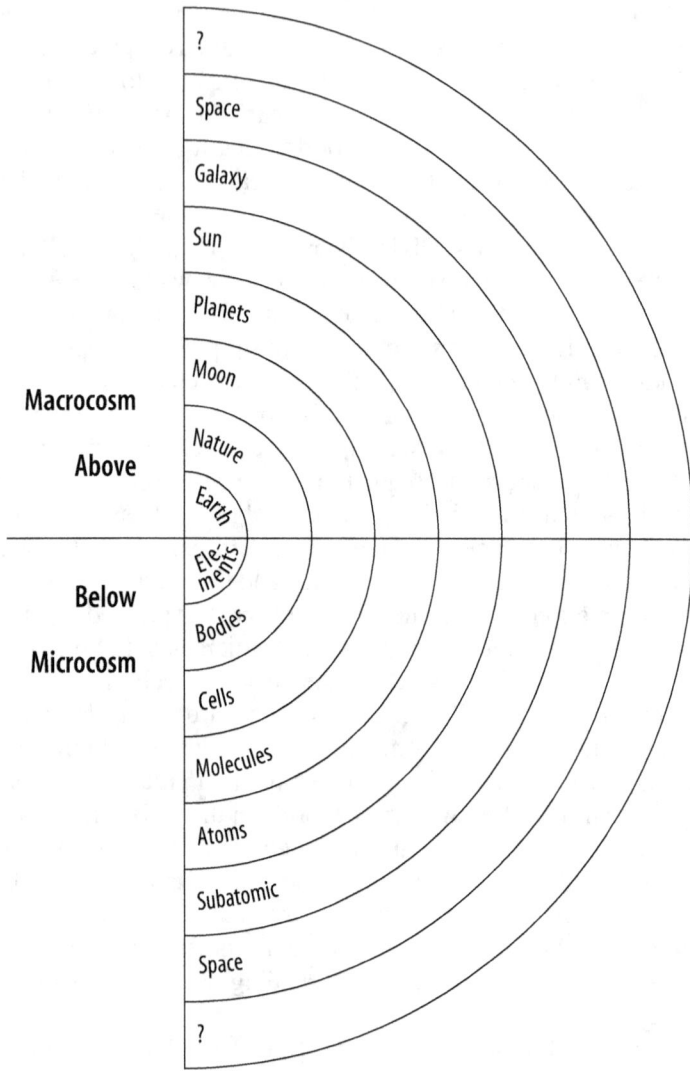

Figure 10—INTERACTION
The esoteric principle of 'As above, so below' is seen here in material terms. The macrocosm and the microcosm resonate, to a greater or lesser degree, with each other. Beyond this physical level, the more subtle fields of the celestial bodies affect humans in particular as they, unlike plants and animals, are not just collective beings but more sensitive individual organisms. An example of this is the wide range of temperaments, talents and levels of consciousness humans can exhibit. Even so they are subject to cosmic rhythms making them sometimes depressed, elated or well balanced in response. (Halevi).

at this level that the subtle planetary principles arise. They do not operate, as many believe, from the physical motions and positions of the planetary bodies. These are merely the material foci in the fourth and lowest World of Action. The planets, in fact, express the sefirotic principles of the highest World in this, the astral level of Existence. Here again, however, is an increased number of laws as the two upper Worlds permeate this third realm. While the greater density makes for a yet more complex World, it is indeed still a very rarefied set of laws compared to those that make up the physical World below.

A way to look at the subtle World, and it is possible for us to do so because it does come within the range of sensual and psychological consciousness, is to observe the mood of a time. History is the human response to these ever-changing subtle cosmic states. Wars and peaceful periods come and go and so do epochs of great expansion or deep depression amongst the nations. Every day the mass media reflect the continuous drama of groups and individuals caught up in this or that breakthrough, development or crisis point. The wheel of fortune favours this project or fails that, brings slow change here and revolution there. Everywhere there is the ebb, ripple and flow of incoming and outgoing tides of events that sometimes flood and occasionally leave dry large areas of humanity while, elsewhere, minute pockets of people are thrust forward or out of the mainstream of history. All this subtle World activity goes on within the general rhythms of Nature, that except for occasional twitches of earthquakes and storms keeps a remarkably regular pattern as the physical Universe slowly turns in its elemental cycle. The difference between the two lowest Worlds is a dimension apart. The stone, plant and animal kingdoms know little or nothing of the subtle and psychological events that preoccupy mankind and, likewise, most of humanity is unaware of the spiritual drama of Creation, let alone the Divine level of Existence.

The bottommost of the four Worlds is the physical. This is quite familiar to us, although we had to learn about it from birth as each incarnating human being has had to do since mankind first came to the Earth. The essence of the physical World is the interplay of matter and energy. These are seen in the Tree of the World of Action, as it is called in Kabbalah, on the two side pillars. Matter is on the left and energy is on the right with the hierarchy of mineral, vegetable, animal and human consciousness running up the central axis.

Seen in another traditional way, the physical World can be set out as a ladder of paired correspondences. Thus the Earth is matched with the elements, the realm of Nature related in miniature with organic bodies, the level of the Moon with the cell, the physical planets with the molecule, the Sun with the atomic realm and the stellar world with the sub-atomic materiality and energy of the galaxies. Beyond the galactic level lies the Greater Space, just as beyond the sub-atomic frontier of the physical World lies the Lesser Space of elemental nothing. This above and below correspondence is one of the mechanisms of resonance applied by the macrocosm upon the microcosm. Such laws and regulations form the basis of astrology.

Taking the planets as an example, we can see how the planetary principles in the subtle World above are manifest in the physical World below in the crude energy and dense matter of the actual planetary bodies, with their surrounding field forces, as they orbit the Sun. Physically these planets are composed of sub-atomic, atomic and molecular force and form and, as such, they have an effect on other bodies composed of a similar energy and materiality. This physical interaction is described precisely by Newton's law that everything has an effect on everything else. The law is applied, however, not only to apples falling to Earth and the Moon's pull and the reciprocal response of the Earth to both but to the particular effect of each of the planets upon the Earth and all those things and creatures within its field-force and upon its surface. The Sun—to take the correspondence further—has a distinct atomic effect and response from the atomic levels of the Earth and its inhabitants. For example, it has been recorded and observed that the rhythm of the gross national product of the United States coincides with the eleven to twenty-two year sunspot and Solar radiation cycle. The galactic level is by far the most subtle of influences. This, we are told, is related to the Great Galactic Year as the Earth changes its position in relation to the Milky Way. This cosmic fluctuation is manifested in the history of mankind as 2,000-year epochs, the present one being the Age of Aquarius. All the foregoing illustrates well the 'As above so below' maxim so often mentioned in ancient Teachings. Now let us examine the 'below' in the nature of man, the microcosm who mimics the chain of interpenetrating Worlds in the four different levels of physical, psychological, spiritual and Divine experience that occupy the same location in time and space in a person. We begin with the physical body, manifested in astrology as the Ascendant.

4. Body and Ascendant

A human being is composed of four different bodies, each one corresponding to the level of reality of each of the four Worlds that make up objective Existence. Most people are totally unaware of anything more than the lowest, physical body and a little of the psychological organism that creates their moods. The reason for this is that they are at the first stage of human evolution and have no conscious memory of a descent from the upper Worlds, as they have no recollection of being in the womb of their mother. The significance of this state is complex and can only be grasped by some understanding of the true nature of a human being and its position in the four Worlds. This is acquired by the study of oneself. The first step is an examination of the physical human body.

The physical body is an elemental machine run on the relationship between solids, liquids, gases and heat, or Earth, Water, Air and Fire. While the mechanism is organic in origin it cannot function without these elemental interactions and all the pipes, valves, chambers, pumps and numerous bits of biological mechanism that go to make up the physical body. So the first level of man is in fact a mineral base with some metallic traces in the matter and energy exchange that holds the body together as a piece of operational machinery from birth to death. Any major functional breakdown causes the mechanism to cease working, just like any other engine.

The second level is the chemical. This operates through the organ systems, like the renal or blood circulation, and through the tissue that composes the fabric of the body. The chemical metabolism of the body is crucial to its efficiency and state. For example, the physical inclination towards passive or active tendencies will develop depending upon whether the anabolic or katabolic side is predominant. This is well illustrated in the day-to-day sense of well- or ill-being and, over a long period, by the gradually shifting bodily moods of lethargy or enthusiasm for life. These periods all have a connection with astrological factors. Firstly, the day-by-day rhythms are affected by the Earth's rotation and the Moon's position which influences the body fluids and their chemical reactions. For example, it has been discovered that blood coagulates at different speeds according to the quarter of the Moon. The longer periods are governed by planetary positions and aspects. One theory is that each planet has a definite effect on a distinct member of the glandular system of the body. Thus Mercury and Venus affect the thyroid and parathyroid endocrine glands, stimulating and restraining the body according to their exaltation or detriment; while Jupiter and Saturn govern the posterior and anterior pituitary glands and Neptune the pineal. Mars, it has been suggested, affects the adrenals and Uranus the gonads, with the Sun and Moon governing the thymus and pancreas respectively. This glandular-planetary system is a speculative one. Its value may be in that it identifies the bio-chemical foci that respond to the planets which, in themselves, are macrocosmic manifestations of sefirotic principles in yet higher Worlds.

The next level is the electro-magnetic one. This operates above and within the chemical-molecular level of the hormones and enzymes. The level includes in its scope not only the inter-action of positive and negative ions, upon which the body depends to trigger a million processes, but the electro-magnetic field that enfolds the bio-organism. The presence of this electro-magnetic envelope is conspicuous by its absence at death when only the physical and chemical shell is left. The phenomenon of life, however, is more than a field force of power points and flows. It is also the intermediary between the lowest part of the psyche and the body, much the same as the chemical level is the intermediary between the electronic and the physical levels of the body. From one level it can be perceived as the last detectable physical phenomenon before one deals with pure intelligence while, from another viewpoint, the electro-magnetic field can be seen as the physical basis of the aura that surrounds the living.

Kabbalistically, it is the earthly equivalent to the World of Creation in the microcosm of the body as the chemical and physical bodies are the equivalents of the subtle and physical Worlds. The substance of the field is atomic in that it is composed of electronic force and form, as against the chemical or molecular level of force and form represented by the metabolism. The celestial function of the electro-magnetic level of the body could be said to relate to the Sun which, as a cosmic atomic principle, affects that level of health. Anyone deprived of sunlight for any length of time knows the effect of depleted vitality. Thus the electro-magnetic factor is directly connected to the position of the physical Sun at birth and its consequent progression through the Zodiac. This brings us to our first strictly astrological topic, the Ascendant.

The Ascendant is the body-type of a person, that is whatever sign is in the 1st House gives the flavour or cast to that physical organism. Now, assuming that the reader already has some working knowledge of astrology it will be perceived that, for example, Cancer in the 1st House will give that characteristic pale and smooth Lunar look and watery eye. The face will either be full and round or hooked, each image being the extreme of the Lunar cycle that passes from the thin crescent to the full Moon. From the view of our study, the reason for this is that at the moment of birth the normally fluidic subtle body of the person being incarnated is crystallised into that physical form and its consequent appearance in later life. This means that despite race, nation and family, which contribute to colour, national temperament and family tendency, the person has his own particular astrological mould of features. However, as will be observed, this is very rarely in a pure form because of the other astrological and physical factors, which is why to guess at an Ascendant is not always wise because Mars, for example, which gives a dark sharpness, may well also be in the 1st House and so modify the pale quality of the Lunar face. In another case the Moon, ruler of Cancer, could be heavily afflicted by Saturn, thus hardening the bland quality of the Cancerian features.

Many people consider the Ascendant as of major importance. It is, if a person only lives as a purely physical entity. While it is agreed that indeed most people do just this, it must not be assumed that the Ascendant is ever an overbearing factor. The Ascendant is rather like an astrological bag into which all the biological and psychological equipment and features have been poured. In essence it is the form that the body has been given from birth to fill out within which to act. Thus the Cancerian Ascendant will often be inclined to be fat in later life, be physically sensitive and particularly prone to bodily moods. Moreover, when the physical weaknesses are being considered, the diseases of, say, a Capricorn Ascendant will be of the skin or bone, the Leo of the heart and so on according to the diseases traditionally associated with each sign. The Ascendant is only related to the physical, chemical and electronic levels in the person as the set of the Ascendant crystallises the natural history of that race, nation and family in that particular physical organism.

The physical body is the most dense and complex of the four

Figure 11—MACRO- AND MICROCOSMS
A human being is an image of all the Worlds containing the Divine, Spirit, soul and body in their make-up, whereas the angelics and organic beings can only relate to their respective Worlds. This means that humans have access to the higher Worlds and can be directly influenced by cosmic events. For example, a tense celestial configuration can precipitate a war or economic collapse, as well as generate a Renaissance or Reformation. (Robert Fludd, 17th century).

bodies owned by incarnate man. It has been evolved over millions of years and is governed right down to its minutest detail of electronic fluctuations by the weight of all the laws of the upper Worlds, as well as its own terrestrial ones. There is, in fact, very little flexibility in the body in relation to the cosmic environment. A few dozen degrees of heat or cold beyond the small norm of our planetary conditions will destroy the body. This very crucial zone in which organic life can support itself indicates just how critical is the balance between terrestrial conditions and celestial influence. It also illustrates how, at the moment of birth, that sign which is coming up to the Eastern horizon has the effect of a cosmic bow-wave upon the ship being launched. The cutting or leading edge of the celestial influence of the Ascendant strikes the baby's body as it comes out of the womb. More potent than any other physical conditions present at birth, it acts like a seashore wave that washes up, arranges the sand into a particular pattern and withdraws, leaving the sand to dry and harden. The patterns, moreover, are not random but twelve basic layouts with modifications of celestial influence.

The Ascendant may be seen as the result of the blend of a terrestrial and celestial moment of interaction. Astrologically, it determines how the person appears to the outer world and how he reacts physically. To judge by the characteristics of the Ascendant is a very superficial assessment. However, it must be taken into account because it is indeed the point of meeting between the outer and the inner Worlds which, consciously or unconsciously, influence our lives and the way we respond and are responded to. The Ascendant is not unlike the clothes we wear to indicate our type and position, except that the Ascendant, the coat of skin as the Bible calls it, is given its astrological style by forces that determine our exact moment of birth. This moment is in no way accidental. It is a delicately manipulated event designed within the ever-changing cosmic fluctuations to bring that particular person fully into the body and locked in at a particular time. This moment of cosmic and earthly fusion fashions the psyche and imprints upon the flesh, which carries inbred tendencies of parents, people and race, the Ascendant overlay that will make the person an instinctive thinker, feeler or doer, be a thin nervous ectomorph, a soft, inclined-to-fat, sensitive endomorph or a muscular and ever-active mesomorph. These characteristics flow out of, or rather into, the mould set up by the signs, planets and luminaries affecting the Ascendant. The proof of this is that while there are physical family characteristics which are passed on, not every child is a replica of its parent. However, if there is a striking similarity it can usually be traced to the family's astrological makeup which is often interlinked by the laws of fate. But before we can begin to discuss the nature of fate we must study and understand the makeup of the psyche which is the prime generator of a life pattern.

5. *Planetary Body*

The psyche is the modern name for what used to be called the sidereal or planetary body. It is the subtle anatomy of a human being and corresponds to the greater World of Formation or the subtle level of reality. While the psyche's structure is based upon the same model as the physical body, its operations are not like the mechanical or organic processes found in organic matter. However, it is similar in that it follows the same set of principles that emanated from the first World that came into existence before the beginning of Time. Using the model of the sefirotic Tree we will set out the structure and dynamics of the psyche or planetary body.

Starting with the bottommost sefirah of the planetary Tree we see, according to the Jacob's Ladder, how this is where the subtle body is locked into the physical Tree below. Here meet the cell tissue of the brain and the central nervous system, the metabolism and the electromagnetic field. This is the psyche's direct connection with the purely material aspect of the body. Above this is the ego mind, that is, that part of us which is partly physical and partly psychological. It belongs to the vegetable level of a man and constitutes the organ of consciousness by which he views the world about him. In man this is a highly sophisticated instrument and forms the foundation of his education, acquired skills, habits, memory and image of himself. It is the ordinary mind, the day-by-day level of awareness by which he finds his way about and does all the habitual things he needs to do in order to survive in the environment and in relation to other people. If the body at the base of the Tree represents the Ascendant and the planet Earth, then the ego is seen to pair with the principle of the Moon.

Now as the Moon has two sides so has the ego, the light and the dark. These positive and negative aspects show themselves in friendly and hostile attitudes based on the acquired education of the ego. This does not have to be seen in terms of school or college education but in life in general, so that the Moon-like quality of the ego reflects the image built up over the years. The dark side of the psychological Moon is that part of the ego that does not reveal itself, either because it does not wish to or considers its views socially unacceptable because the Moon-ego is socially-oriented: its image in its society and to itself being all important.

A little contemplation upon the link between the Moon and the ego will reveal much. The waxing and waning moods of the ego are a precise parallel to a person's experience of his natal Moon. For example it will be observed, by more sensitive people, that when the current Lunar position is square or in opposition to their natal Moon, tension is experienced, as is ease when trines and sextiles occur. This, of course, is only a general rule applying to this level of the psyche. What is important is to see the differentiation between the bodily state of the Ascendant and the moods of the ego. Here can be observed two interpenetrating spheres of influence: the physical Moon's phases acting upon the Ascendant body and upon the ego as defined by the natal Moon.

The next level is a frontier zone between the physical and the psychological. The sefirot corresponding to Mercury and Venus represent those principles in the subtle body that act as biopsychological functions. Here there is an important distinction to be made between the first seven planets (including Earth) and the luminaries (see Figure 12). The planets set on the side pillars operate as the active and passive functions in the Solar system. This cannot be seen directly in the macrocosm but can easily be observed in the parallel system in the psychological or interior Solar system. Take, for example, the two we are examining. Mercury is at the reflective position. It responds, carries messages, tunes and carries out a myriad of duties to inform the psyche of what the other principles or gods are doing in that World; while on the active station, the principle corresponding with Venus stimulates input, circulates energy, pumps, arouses and vitalises the bio-psychological zone which, together with its complementary Mercurial sefirah, it occupies. The Venus position on the active pillar is often queried by people who do not look beyond astrological clichés. Venus is the active female and any young woman at the period of Venus in her life knows, as do her admirers, that it is she who takes the real initiative in most situations. Venus is the driving power behind passion while Mercury is the fast but delicate, ever-moving butterfly, always drawn but never leading action. At this level they represent a multi-rôled inferior planetary system which is concerned with meeting the needs of body, the ego and the Self which is hidden in the unconscious level of the person.

PLANETARY BODY   49

At the centre of the Tree of the psyche is the Self. This is the Sun of the inner Solar system. While being a luminary like the Moon, it represents a higher level of consciousness because, unlike the Moon which only reflects, it generates light. This Self is the centre of the psyche, the essence of the individual. While a person's ego-mind may be educated into this or that image of a rich man or a poor man, a fool or a wise man, the Self is nothing but itself. It is recognised as the lucid watcher in dreams or the one who occasionally looks on with an impartial eye during a major crisis or moment of deep peace. It is the honest part of oneself that sometimes speaks with a quiet authority when the ego is about to do something stupid but perhaps socially acceptable. Generally speaking the Self remains in the background of a man's life, in his unconscious, beyond the veil that stretches between Mercury and Venus. This line on the psychological Tree is the threshold across which experience passes going into store in the memory banks of the planetary body. This liminal line is the frontier of the unconscious across which come the responses from deep within the psyche. The Sun stands behind this veil, sometimes guiding by proxy and sometimes awaiting to be called directly when the ego-Moon cannot cope with a new and crucial situation. This is because the Self is primarily concerned with the truth about a life. Like the Sun's god, Apollo, it can only see truth and few ego-Moons can face the Self's direct rays. From an astrological point of view, the Zodiacal position of the Sun in the chart determines the particular quality of the Self and its position in the mundane House points out the area of life in which the Self is meant to operate, should it ever come into its own. However, most people live off either their Ascendant or Moon. This will be dealt with later in detail.

The positions of the planets Mars and Jupiter are occupied by the psychological sefirot concerned with the emotional life of a person. This level is quite distinct from the feelings and moods which are usually the result of the inferior planets, the Moon and the Ascendant working upon the psycho-biological processes, the ego-mind and the body. The emotional level of the psyche is much more rarely manifest than most people imagine. The deep love or bitter quarrel that lasts for months or years rather than days belong to this order. So, too, do the phenomena of remorse, conscience and courage as well as a love of one's work, religious devotion or even righteous anger. All these emotions, some good and some bad, are of this planetary level and shake and stir the psyche profoundly at certain periods of life when

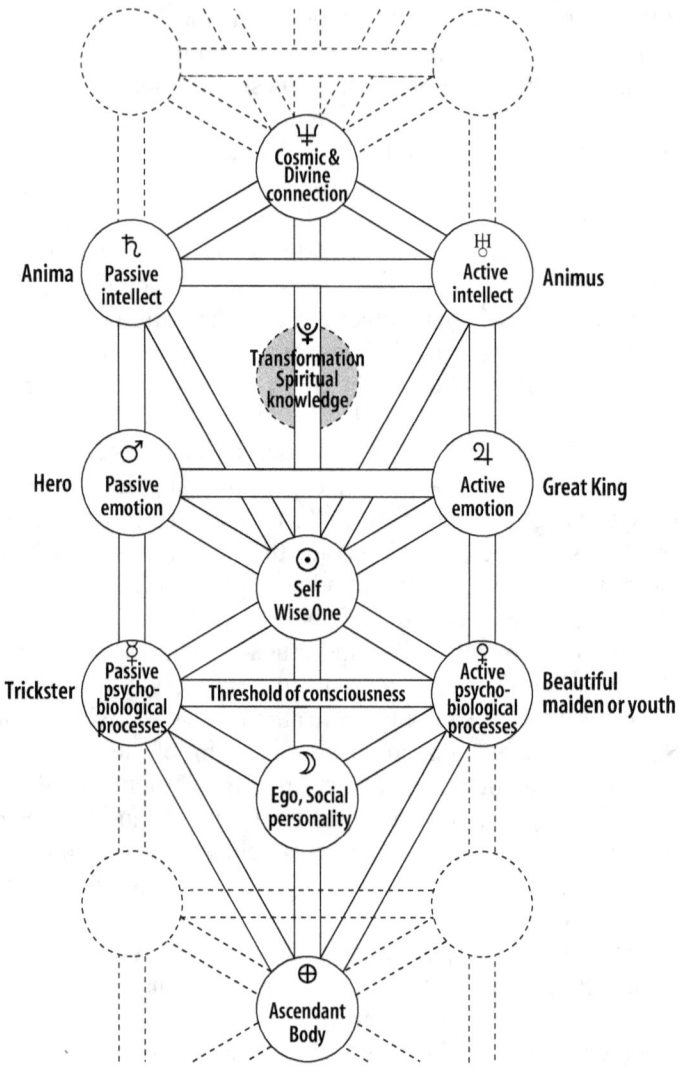

Figure 12 — SYMBOLISM
In this scheme we have, besides the planetary archetypes, the symbols of Jungian psychology. This is because the psyche is of the same nature and substance as the celestial realm, whereas the body is of the Earth and subject to its laws. Here Mercury, for example, is the Trickster, or the quick mental processes of the ordinary mind, while Venus, as the sexual drive of psycho-biological activity, manifests in the Femme Fatale *or* Casanova. *The superior planets, for most people, are in the unconscious. Most heroes are oblivious to the Martial force that motivates them, as is the genius of Uranus.* (Halevi).

Mars or Jupiter are well or badly placed. This, in many Traditions, is the place of the soul, or that part of ourselves which is concerned with more than daily life. Mars and Jupiter are sometimes seen as the guardian angels who watch over the moral aspects of the psyche.

Seen in kabbalistic terms, the question is often asked: why is Mars on the passive column? The answer is that, as the reverse of the active Venus, Mars is the passive, constraining side to the active principle. It is emotional power under discipline. No soldier is a soldier unless he is in control. The whole basis of martial arts is to know when to start and when to stop. The usual picture of Mars as the violent warrior is a good example of the degeneration of a very important principle.

Jupiter is seen as a great and generous King, full of power and active compassion as against Mars's strict justice. These images bring in the psychological archetypes observed by C. G. Jung. In Jung's scheme will be seen the psychological reflection of the planetary gods. Thus the Mercury principle is seen as the archetype of the Trickster, Venus as the archetype of the beautiful youth or maiden, Mars and Jupiter as the archetypes of the Hero and the great King. The Moon is the person's archetypal image of himself and the Sun archetype is sometimes called the Wise One. Above, on the psychological Tree where Saturn and Uranus are to the left and right, are the archetypes of the Anima and the Animus, or the Great Mother and Father figures.

The upper pair of Saturn and Uranus represent the deep intellectual processes of the psyche. Saturn is the slow pondering of understanding, or reason, while Uranus represents the sudden flash of illumination. Both these processes are usually hidden in the unconscious of most people and only let their findings be known when these two superior planets are particularly critically placed, as for instance when Saturn returns to its original natal position or Uranus comes into precise opposition to the natal Uranus. Saturn has the effect of taking stock of the last and the next thirty years and the Uranus crisis usually precipitates a profound shock to all previous patterns, to show the good and bad fruit they have borne. Both planets' influence within the psyche is more easily recognised by anyone over thirty years of age, for Saturn, and over forty for Uranus. Seen from another viewpoint, one could say that these two outer planets represent the cosmic frontier of a natural man's psyche, the furthest and deepest he is capable of comprehending while still only concerned with just the Natural World. He may acquire understanding and even have revelation but unless he has developed a supernatural capability which opens out the cosmic aspects of Saturn and Uranus, he is confined to the lower subtle and physical Worlds in his appreciation of the Universe and its workings.

The two outermost planets of Neptune and Pluto, which are just beyond the reach of the unaided eye (a significant fact), occupy a strange position on the Tree. While the stations are speculative, as is Uranus for the present, it looks, according to findings by perceptive astrologers, as though they represent the fourth level or the manifestation of the highest Worlds beyond the ordinary psyche. By this is meant that they are, for mankind at large, so remote that their effect is general rather than particular. This reasoning is backed up by the simple astronomical fact that both these distant planets move at a relatively very slow pace, so slow that they can only have a fractional or vague effect on an individual life. Their influence is more, it would seem, on a scale of generations and of history than a single life's span. This places them, as suggested by their position on the Tree of Formation, in contact with the upper Trees of Creation and Emanation on Jacob's Ladder. As such they perform as the intermediaries, in their remote stations in the Solar system, to the Galaxy and beyond. Considered from these upper and outermost Worlds, their orbital spheres are the first two that galactic influence has to pass through as it enters the Solar system. Pluto and Neptune, as psychological principles, relate to the collective unconscious and the individual unconscious respectively, Pluto representing the direct connection with the cosmic or spiritual level of Existence and Neptune the connection with the World of Emanation and its Divine Presence. These lie far beyond the perception of most people and therefore have little relevance to the general psychological frame of reference. But more on these two planets later.

Perceived as a whole, the planetary body is a delicately balanced anatomy. It is a subtle organism whose lowest parts are enmeshed in the physical body by its Earth, Moon, Mercury and Venus principles. It has an emotional level in its middle zone comprising the Mars-Sun-Jupiter triad, an upper intellectual level governed by the Saturnine and Uranian principles and a connection with the spiritual and Divine Worlds above through Pluto and Neptune. These four basic levels are the interior manifestation in a human being of the great Solar system of the subtle World. As such they not only correspond in astral level to the planets and luminaries but respond to any fluctuations that occur in that sidereal realm. This makes the human being who is unaware of his full situation subject to external influences he might otherwise resist or even make use of in his favour, for it is only possible to utilise these subtle conditions if one is aware of the forces at work around and within one. Alas, for most people only the forces of the Earth, Moon and inferior planets have any real meaning. Living under the regulations of the vegetable and animal levels there is, to quote the Bible, 'Nothing new under the Sun.' This expression takes on its full significance when there is a recognition of the invisible and unconscious upper Worlds above the Sun when seen in terms of the kabbalistic Tree. Until then, the effect of the superior planets and the Worlds beyond are only general as people are moved *en masse* into fashions, emigrations, wars and social revolutions and the like. The study of such general events is the concern of Mundane Astrology. This is the concern of our next chapter.

6. Mundane Astrology

By now we should be aware that the Universe is composed of four levels of reality: the Worlds of physical Action, subtle Formation, cosmic Creation and Divine Emanation. We should also be acquainted with the notion that a human being has in his microcosmic organism four corresponding levels, namely a carnal body, a subtle or planetary body and the presence of spiritual and Divine levels deep within the psyche. The correspondence of the same kinds of reality is the key to the astrological relationship between the greater and lesser Worlds of the macrocosm and man. However, while there is the connection, the degree of direct influence varies according to the stage of evolution of a person. Thus for example, a man who lives only for food and propagation comes primarily under the laws and influence of the physical World. This mechanical level of astrology is the lowest and most general form of mundane fate. Let us examine its mechanism and implication.

Like the beginning of Existence, the World of the elements and action emerges out of No-thing, according to physicists, in the form of minute impulses of energy or packets of matter. This manifestation of the physical World is the last stage of the four-World process of descent from the Divine to the mundane. From this point on, the process of ascent or evolution begins as physical energy and matter begin to be organised out of their most primitive and least intelligent states into more complex and sensitive organisations. The first phase is the birth of the hydrogen atom which is the simplest element in the Universe. This gas, we are told, appears out of nowhere and fills the vastness of physical space. Whether the Big Bang or Steady State Universe theories are correct is not directly relevant here because energy and matter undoubtedly begin with hydrogen. The next stage was the conversion of the simple hydrogen atom into helium. This was and is still being brought about by the compression and nuclear fission of hydrogen in the midst of dense and massive clouds of gas that collect and swirl about in vortices called nebulae. The result of the atomic activity so generated was the creation of a two-electron helium atom which precipitated a process that escalated, over billions of years, to produce a physical Universe composed of many elements. Out of this began to evolve the next stage, that is, molecular materiality.

Taking our own Solar system as an example, the atomic Sun was created out of the gaseous nebula of the Milky Way and from the nuclear processes of Solar evolution was formed the molecular planetary system that now orbits the Sun. The situation, at this present point of evolution, is that the planets have evolved a stage further, so that they not only have atomic and electronic substance and fields but each has an internal exchange of chemical action and materiality. Taking our own Earth, at least one planet has progressed a phase on from the purely mineral level of existence to be able to support organic life. This web of cellular consciousness spread round the Earth's sphere is held between the liquid and solid elements below and the gaseous and radiant envelopes above. As an integral part of the Earth, organic life is a highly sensitive skin which both receives and radiates cosmic energy, substance and consciousness. Of terrestrial outgoings science knows little but of the celestial incomings a little observation of the yearly cycle and some contemplation of natural history will establish the effects of the macrocosm upon the Earth. Besides the obvious turn of the seasons in response to the Sun and the Moon's effect upon growth patterns there is, for instance, the effect of the eleven to twenty-two year Solar cycle upon the grape harvests, the increase and decrease of certain diseases and the rhythm of world trade. On a greater scale there are the long range weather fluctuations, the oscillating sea levels and the periodic ice ages. All these phenomena and many more are due to the Earth's crucial position in the Solar system where it is held in delicate balance between the Sun, the planets and the Moon. A few millions of miles away from or towards the Sun would change the character of the Earth and its present ability to receive and impart cosmic influences.

The concept of extraterrestrial influence is closer now to acceptance in the so-called orthodox body of knowledge than it has ever been, if only because the discovery of the radio Universe in this century made scientists realise that there is a whole aspect of physical creation that has been totally unknown to natural man. To the supernatural or evolved man the discovery of the radio emissions of Jupiter, for example, was of no surprise. Pythagoras, it is said, was able actually to perceive the signals and intelligent astrologers down the ages have accepted the concept of celestial interaction at this level as a major factor in their philosophy.

The Solar system is a highly complex set of checks and balances with the various planets of different sizes and compositions orbiting the Sun at different distances and speeds. This is the physical base of a very subtle cosmic organisation. Taking a step back into deep space, we may perhaps glimpse the Solar system as a complete organism if we can break our normal Earth-oriented standpoint. The Solar system is travelling at a considerable speed round the disc of the Milky Way. Seen from our deep space position it would appear, in the galactic time scale, to be like a kind of cosmic firefly with the planets weaving a series of orbital sheaths round the glowing spine of the Sun as it moves towards the star Vega. Such a cosmic entity was perceived as a creature, as a god, by the ancient visionaries who saw themselves as existing inside the body of the Solar system much as the cells live within the body of a man. Indeed, the analogy was taken yet further with the Sun seen as the heart and the planets viewed as the organs of the body of the Solar system. The Earth, for instance, was considered as a most delicate planetary organ governing the health of the Solar system, rather like the human skin that is continually being born and dying as it serves our physical organism. The notion of the Solar system being a living entity in its own right is not so strange as it appears at first sight when we consider the bacteria within our bodies and how we are the equivalent bacteria to the Earth. There is a law that the greater World always contains the lesser and so on up and down the ladder of Existence. This brings us to the realisation that the Solar system itself as a whole is subject to galactic influence—and science is aware of this in the presence of cosmic waves and particles that pass from the centre of the Milky Way, clear through the Solar system and Earth and out to the galactic rim, perhaps to affect other galaxies like Andromeda which is millions of light years away. Here we must remember that for each level of Existence there is a different time and space scale. Thus, for certain cells our day is a lifetime, while for us the Solar pulse beat is twenty-two years of our incarnation. This oscillation of the Sun, however, is nothing to the Milky Way whose time scale reduces the Sun's long life to the equivalent of a brief stellar cell's lifespan within the Galaxy's vast body.

Having set out the scale of the physical scheme we can now examine, bearing in mind the above factors, the real meaning of mundane astrology. Firstly, mundane astrology by definition refers to general fate: that is, the world-wide response to cosmic influence. Let us begin with the most physical sense of the subject. According to natural historians, the planet Earth has passed through many stages of evolution. First came the various mineral phases which were created by fire; then water formed rocks, the latter being the subtler levels of the mineral kingdom. Next came the organic stage with the vegetable kingdom literally preparing the ground for the animal, because the animal cannot feed directly upon the mineral level. These latter stages divide into greater and greater complexity and subtlety, not only because of the species spontaneously evolving but also due to the needs of the planet and the changes of incoming cosmic influence. The principle is simple; a plant can absorb and retain more radiation than a stone and an animal can respond to a wider spectrum of influence than a plant. Thus evolution meets the Earth's desire for finer and more efficient organisms to act as its skin and external organs. In this way there evolved a series of plants and animals that became dominant, like the great coal ferns and the dinosaurs, for millions of years and then lost place to the more subtle and developed plants and animals of later epochs. These early species died out on the planet in the same way that the human tail eventually withered in the body and became the ossified coccyx. This is the largest scale of mundane astrology.

The next level is the appearance of man on the planet. Here was created a species of life that contained all that had gone before. Man had the mineral, vegetable and animal principles within him so that, together with his additional consciousness, he could serve the planet better than any other terrestrial creature. However, mankind on the whole began as vegetable human beings confined to one place like plants, not venturing beyond their immediate habitat. Later, when mankind evolved beyond its defenceless status into a hunting culture, it became the human animal with tribal or herd instincts. In this evolutionary stage there was little individuality and people lived according to the social pressures of tribal custom and survival situation. All the influences were external, which is to say that they were governed by Nature which, in turn, was ruled by the stage of the planet's weather—for example, the ice or tropical ages—which in its turn was influenced by the state of the Solar system and so on.

It was only with the birth of nations, that is something bigger than the direct blood connection of the tribe, that a newer, subtler influence manifested. It was at this point that astrology proper was conceived

Figure 13 — EARTH AND THE HEAVENS
The influence of the Sun and Moon is clearly apparent but not that of the planets. Over time, as observations were correlated, it became clear that not only did the positions of the planets in the Zodiac have an effect but so did their place at any given moment in relation to each other. Moreover, as the Sun is at its most potent at sunrise and noon, so was any planet on the Ascendant and Midheaven of the birth chart. This made it possible to predict the effect on certain Earthly conditions. For example, it seemed wise to start any business venture when Mercury was in Gemini. This was how Mundane Astrology was born. (16th century woodcut).

because by then the long rhythms and crucial incidents of a people's history had been recorded and studied. It was perceived, for example, that nations, like flowers, were born, bloomed, faded and even died. It was also noted that when a nation was created out of a confederation of tribes that it took on a particular character which could be related to what was known about the human temperament born at the same time of year. Moreover, if the actual date of the creation of a people was not known, then it could be guessed at intelligently by sensitive observers with astrological knowledge. Thus, in the ancient world the nations were given zodiacal signs, even though their founding dates were unknown. For example, Imperial Rome was accorded Leo while the traditionally-minded Jews were seen as Capricornian. In later times the moment when a state was born was not only recorded but 'elected,' that is, carefully chosen. England is an example—William the Conqueror had himself crowned at noon on Christmas Day in 1066, thus giving that country the Capricornian respect for law and the political longevity it has enjoyed for nearly a thousand years. The birth of the United States is another case in point. Its constitution was not only formulated by colonial English gentry but also not without some thought, by its Masonically-trained founders, of the timing of the birth of the nation. The actual moment of the signing of the Declaration of Independence at 3.04 a.m. on 4 July 1776 in Philadelphia was not casual. In the chart is embodied the American dream. This example is ideal to illustrate the essence of Mundane Astrology in detail.

To begin with, the American chart has a Gemini Ascendant which will give it the physical characteristic of duality. The American schism of nineteenth-century North and South with its Civil War and the East and West coast cultures demonstrate the twin aspect of the country. The Sun in Cancer also prefigures a nation composed of many states, peoples and religions. Indeed, there is no other country in the world that is such an amalgam of all the races under one constitution. White, black, yellow and red live together, although the Mars in Gemini and on the Ascendant indicates conflict of brother with brother. The Sun in the 2nd House, along with Mercury, indicates great natural wealth and commercial acumen which has been borne out by American history. Venus in the 1st House indicates the American style of hospitality and generosity in first meetings, despite the very materialistic factor of the Sun which would strongly favour a capitalistic economy of Cancerian 'me and mine.' The Aquarian Moon, however, would illustrate the American idealism with its position

USA: 3.04a.m. 4 July 1776 Philadelphia, Pennsylvania, USA.

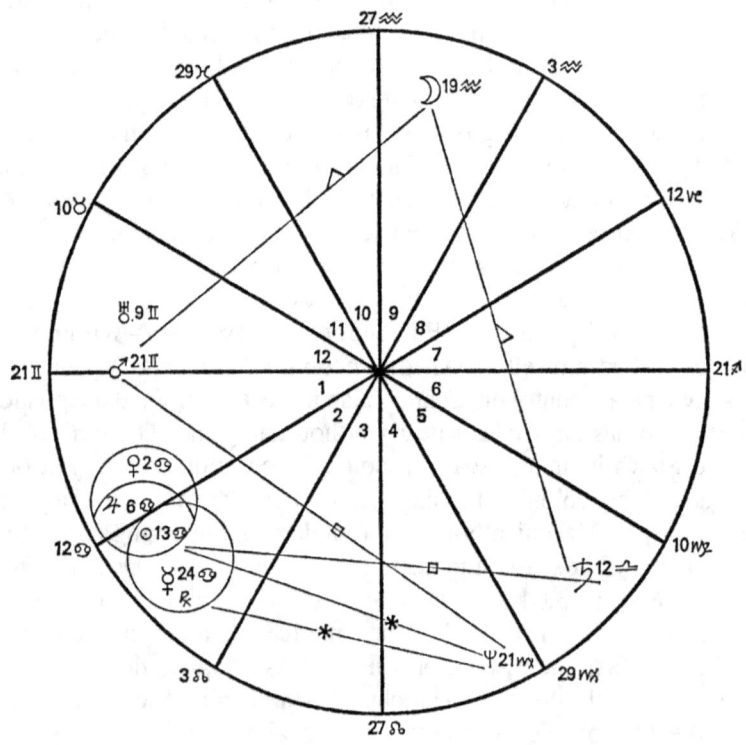

Figure 14 — HOROSCOPE OF THE USA
This was drawn up for the moment when, after a long debate, the Declaration of Independence was signed. It was then that the United States came into being. One critical element in this mundane chart is Mars right on the Ascendant, indicating it had been born out of conflict between brothers, as it is in Gemini. This was summed up by a British statesman of the time, who said, 'This war is between Englishmen fighting Englishmen over the rights of Englishmen.' It also foreshadowed the Civil War later, between Northern and Southern states. (Halevi).

in this democratically-minded sign in the 9th House. Here the Moon created the anti-colonial and anti-aristocratic image America has of itself, despite its Solar self-interest as demonstrated in its great international business corporations that take other nations' resources into its very Cancerian commercial domain. Moreover, the Sun-squared Saturn in Libra in the 5th House bodes a heavy imperial hand on its dependants and partners but the Saturn trine to the Moon alleviates this and helps the United States retain some of its idealism. Neptune in the 4th House of security indicates deception and corruption in domestic matters which is where the finer focus of mundane examination will come into sharpness as we look at a particular epoch in American history to illustrate an example of mundane celestial and terrestrial influence and response.

In August 1973 Saturn entered Cancer. It did not leave that sign until June 1976. During the period that the planet of suffering and learning was passing through America's Sun sign, the nation suffered its first military defeat in Vietnam, had its most scandalous revelations about government, went through its worst economic depression for several decades and had its President resign in disgrace, a thing that had never happened before. Moreover, 1976 was the bi-centennial year of its existence. The astrological reasons for these events are very precise. During this epoch Saturn, having conjoined the American Ascendant, then eclipsed the natal Mars (thus impairing its military effort in Vietnam) then passed through the 1st House to leave its sobering mark upon the United States' appearance or reputation in the world. There it then transited the natal Venus and Jupiter, thus constraining the two benifics which depressed the nation's economic position and created unemployment for a while. Saturn then went on to conjoin the American Sun, that is the principle of truth, and here the national disgrace of the Watergate security scandal emerged because Saturn, besides being the hard teacher, is also the planet of justice and law. The fall of President Nixon is equally astrologically prefigured.

Richard Nixon (January 9, 1913—April 22, 1994) was a Capricorn and Saturn was his planetary ruler. Saturn in its opposite sign of Cancer is in its detriment and thus the nation's humiliation and the President's forced resignation coincided just as Saturn transited, on 8 August 1974, in the exact and original Solar position of thirteen degrees of Cancer. Nixon's natal Sun in eighteen degrees of Capricorn got the full negative impact a little while later in shock as Saturn entered into full opposition to his natal Sun. He nearly died.

Now we have seen how terrestrial events below correspond to celestial events above and how precise the interaction can be. This, of course, can be applied to great and small matters but it is most important to realise, as regards mundane astrology, that the general events contain, for most of humanity, the particular. By this is meant, for example, that many American soldiers who fought and died in the Vietnam war were caught up in national events that over-rode their possibility of individual fate. They, like most people, lived according to the external pressures of social and tribal custom except those, for example, who as individuals risked public disgrace and avoided being drafted into the army. Here again, however, one must look deeper because, while some were genuine conscientious objectors to the war, there was a number of draft avoiders who followed a developing anti-war trend in America that was generated by the same Saturn transit. Saturn is the planet of understanding and long-term view and anyone who wants to survive has this in their outlook.

The gradually unfolding history of various nations in relation to one another is the concern of mundane astrology. That is, the pattern of general human development is as subject to a celestial climate as the terrestrial weather and earthquakes. Indeed, the human and elemental levels often express, each in their own way, the same cosmic tension. An example of this was the massive conjunction in Leo of the Sun, Moon, Saturn, Venus and Mercury squared to Uranus in Scorpio in July 1976. This heavenly impact point precipitated major earthquakes in several countries: one Chinese city counted over 250,000 dead. On the more subtle side, the disruptive innovative planet of Uranus in the hidden but violent sign of Scorpio, squared to the repressive conservative planet of Saturn in the imperial sign of Leo, triggered by the Truth of the Sun and the mass impulser of the Moon, brought about an unusual civil and racial outburst in authoritarian countries like the Republic of South Africa, the reversal of a white supremist policy in Rhodesia indicating the end of a colonial epoch, the death of Mao Tse-Tung, China's communist emperor and its subsequent political and social changes and rebellion, the highly symbolic assassination of the British Ambassador in Dublin by the Irish Republican Army and the spontaneous rise of the Irish peace movement to end the long urban guerilla war. All these are excellent examples of the disruptive Uranus when squared to the imperial power of the sign of Leo.

Looking from the Worlds above, the celestial mechanics of such events are most interesting. As the planets move around the Solar system they undergo stresses and eases as their bodies and field-forces conjoin, oppose and angle each other. These geometric relationships fall into three main classifications: tense, neutral and relaxed. An analogue which illustrates the principle well is a room full of people who continuously pass and relate to each other in a friendly, indifferent or hostile manner. When there is an unusual set of planetary relationships there is usually an exceptional response created upon the Earth. These either temporarily disrupt the balance of the regular rhythms and give rise to wars and natural disasters or focus in such a way as to precipitate particularly unusual events that might take years to manifest, like the birth of a civilisation. A traditional example was when many planets aligned themselves into one part of the sky so closely that they appeared to be a single star. This meant that the planets formed a long axis of celestial power in the Solar system which generated an event of extraordinary potency. Such a lineup of planets is described by the Star of Bethlehem which reached its maximum point of conjunction over one place at a certain time, then to disperse, a theoretically unrepeatable astrological focus of cosmic power. Whether this event actually occurred is perhaps relevant only to the Christian astrologer. However, the principle is correct and many less perfect examples of planetary alignment in history prove that such moments and configurations are highly significant. One such major conjunction of planets occurred on 4 February 1962. That was the world-crisis year when the United States and Russian military confronted each other over Cuba and China and India fought each other in the Himalayas. Four of the world's most populous nations were at the brink of what would have become global and atomic war. It was a crucial turning point for the human race at that time and the threat of mass nuclear destruction receded for over a decade.

On the wider scale we still await the unfolding of the conjunction's long-term implications. From the point of view of our study, such a moment would have a profound influence on the generation born at the time when five planets and the Sun were in Aquarius, particularly those whose birth was on the day when the Moon also conjoined the configuration. The effect of this maximum focus on the subsequent lives has yet to be seen in terms of individual fate and cosmic destiny. But before we can examine such matters we must try to understand the subtle as well as the physical processes of conception, gestation and birth into the flesh.

7. Descent into Flesh

An analogue of how the celestial World influences the terrestrial situation can be seen in the effect of musical notes upon a plate sprinkled with very fine powder. Experiments show that various frequencies produce the phenomenon of distinct patterns in the dust that alter as the notes are raised, lowered or played in different combinations. In viewing such sequences one sees the powder arrange itself into a flowing series of intricate formations that take up a wide variety of shapes and speeds according to the harmonies, disharmonies, violence or gentleness of the sound. It is like observing a concerto in solid form. If one perceives the same principle on a greater scale, one thinks of a similar process occurring in relation to the music of the spheres where the effect of the luminaries, planets and stars influence the ever-changing flow of forms of the terrestrial scene as it responds to the celestial orchestra.

Still using the above analogue, it is also noted that if the sound input is stopped, then the powder freezes in the pattern of that moment. This gives us a clue of what might happen when a discarnate psyche is removed from the direct influences of the subtle World, is fixed in a solid body of flesh and blood and comes under the rulership of physical laws. Bearing this notion of crystallisation in mind, let us go back beyond the moments of birth and conception so that we can perceive how the three Worlds of cosmic Creation, subtle Formation and physical Action make up a chain of descending causes and effects. This should help us to understand the processes that bring about the natal horoscope.

Ancient Tradition says that after the Universe had been created it was filled initially with basically three kinds of creatures. Seen in terms of the four Worlds, those 'below' moved and had their being in the bottom two Worlds, those of Formation and Action, and had physical bodies, while those 'above' moved in the two middle Worlds of Creation and Formation. The two classes, we are told, generally could not intrude into the others' territory. The third class of beings brought into existence were unique creatures because they could

DESCENT INTO FLESH 65

traverse all the three lower Worlds. This was mankind. The topmost World was not, at this point, included in the plan because here was the Divine Zone into which only those who had experienced all levels of Existence could be admitted. This was to be the prize for the most perfected in the great cosmic drama, in which God should behold God.

Thus it is said that Adam, the image of God, was called into existence and that out of the Divine Will was created the cosmic Spirit of humanity. This great Spiritual Adam, Tradition goes on to say, then divided, as it descended into the World of Forms, into the male and female souls. In terms of our four Worlds, all the spirits that compose mankind pre-existed before they became souls and all the souls pre-existed before they entered any physical bodies. Thus we have the concept of the spiritual, psychological or subtle and physical or carnal bodies with the Divine potential present deep within. How can this be related astrologically? Let us follow the sequence in detail from the beginning.

Kabbalistic teaching says that the spirit of a person is at first pure and naïve; that it has no other experience than the cosmic World of Creation wherein it was brought into being. Here it resides, with many others who are destined to work with it, until it is required to descend to the subtle World below into what is called the Treasure House of Souls. Here, we are told, the spirit is enclothed in a subtle or a planetary body prior to being incarnated into the flesh. Tradition states that the spirit-soul is very reluctant to descend, because it is quite happy where it is, but it is told that it was created for a special purpose and that it has to pass through the experience of physical existence in order to have a complete knowledge of all the Worlds. Reluctantly the entity descends into birth and soon loses all memory of its prenatal existence although a few, from time to time, do remember something about another life, another World as they occasionally come out of the preoccupations of physical living.

Taking the allegory back to its astrological point of connection, it can be said that the moment of conception, when the two physical parents mate, is when the biological vehicle of the fertilised cell is fused to the bottommost part of the Tree of the Spirit, the centre point of the Tree of the subtle body and the topmost point of the carnal Tree. Here the spirit and the soul are linked to the flesh. From this moment on, the prenatal psyche is slowly immersed in cellular tissue, passing as it does during gestation through all the evolutionary stages of

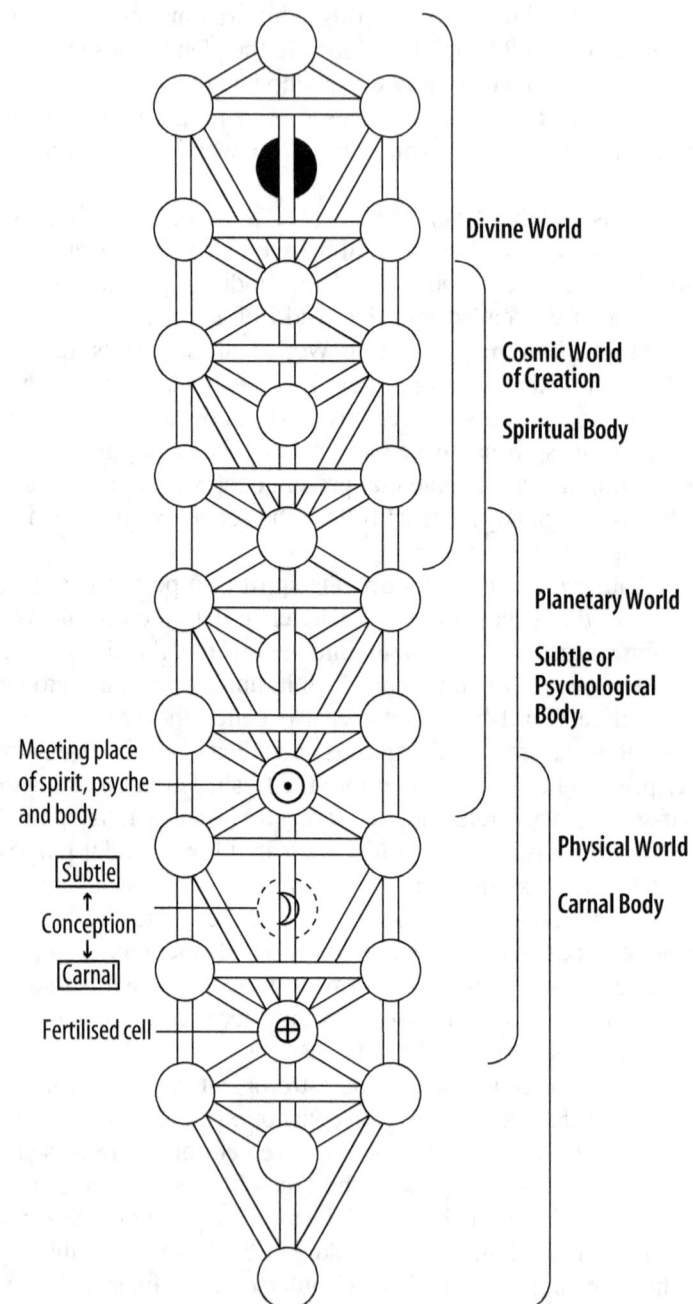

mineral, plant and animal before it becomes a truly human body. Seen kabbalistically, the physical body, based on billions of years of refinement in terrestrial conditions, is slowly invested by the psyche or sidereal body which, in turn, is inhabited by the spirit. The nine months of gestation is a period of the most rapid changes because the process is still largely involved in the World of Formation whose *métier* is constant flow and rearrangement. If the process were just under physical law it would be a slow and crude elemental sequence—which the formation of a child's body certainly is not. The whole operation, to be precise in kabbalistic terms, is one in which all three Worlds of Creation, Formation and Action participate.

During gestation the situation is almost entirely fluid because of the nature of the World it principally occupies. However, it is also at this point in time that the physical characteristics of race, nation and family, initiated by the genes of the parents, act upon the body that is being formed. This is prior to the imprint of the Ascendant. Thus while the family colour, height and purely physical strengths and weaknesses are being imbued during gestation, the particular body type is not. That is to say that although a family may be, say, healthy, its members may be personally lean, muscular or even inclined to fat, as the Ascendant determines at the moment of birth.

The moment of birth comes at the coincidence of two points. The first is the end of the gestation process and the second prime mover is that of subtle World timing. Conception takes place at a particular location and moment in order that a certain entity shall be incarnated into a particular family and circumstance designed for its spiritual development. This occurs on a time scale outside the perception of the sensual World. Perhaps an analogue will help. Imagine that you find a spider in your bath tub. It has crawled up the drain pipe or fallen in. You are about fill the bath. You pause before turning on the hot water and lift the creature out of a death trap and put it somewhere else in the best place for its survival. It scuttles away about its daily business almost totally unaware that it had passed through a fatal encounter. It

---

Figure 15 (Left)—INCARNATION
Conception appears to take place at the level of the Moon which governs the sexual organs and the womb. In reality, it can only occur if the Worlds of Creation, the spirit, the planetary realm of the psyche and that of the body come together to fulfil a cosmic purpose. This happens at the level of the Sun where the three lower Worlds meet to create a physical vehicle for the soul to inhabit. The hour of birth is not random but designed to generate a specific fate for that individual's benefit. (Halevi).

has no knowledge of your kind of intelligence, your moment of judgement and mercy and your consideration of where it should be put. Once it scuttles off under a leaf or ledge it is on its own again, living according to its inherent nature and learnt experience. Your dimension of life has no meaning to the spider. So it is with Providence which oversees the stage-management of Creation from a dimension far beyond most of us. Thus when a human incarnation takes place, it is with profound consideration. Justice and Mercy are exercised to an exact degree. In this way the best survival and growth for that spirit is assured in the subsequent birth and life which will affect both the person and all who come into contact with them.

Up to the first breath, kabbalistic tradition states that the person is aware of the reason for his or her incarnation. The end of the birth is when the first breath is inhaled by the baby and then it becomes not only a separate entity physically from the mother but is fixed out of the fluidity of the subtle World into the solidity of the physical World. From this time on the psyche embedded in the baby's body is held under the additional laws of organic life and begins to forget its prenatal existence. It is now enmeshed, for the lifespan of that cellular and organic vehicle, in the process of growth, maturity, decay and death. This is probably why new born babies cry because it is at the moment they are taken out of the direct flowing influence of the lighter, less bound subtle World that they realise they are imprisoned in the flesh with all its problems. The techniques of gentle birth may alleviate the shock but the impact is still enormous as the entity incarnated seeks, in the comfort of the mother, compensation for the loss of its subtle World freedom.

It is said, again by Tradition, that during the period of gestation the person being incarnated is shown, as a preview, the kind of life he is to live, all the places where he is to go and all the important relationships he is to make. This scenario, we are told, is partially erased at birth because any preconceived notion would affect the factor of free will. However, the general outline of fate is determined. The fate is held as a general pattern so as to fit into the communal fate of that particular family and society, not to mention the wider relationship with that soul's group companions who are incarnated around the same time. These soul kin people the person sometimes recognises on meeting for the first time. He experiences the sense of knowing them from somewhere else. The *déjà vu* phenomenon of coming into a place that seems familiar also belongs to the prenatal view of fate.

Providence, whose meaning is foresight, provides a clue to the life plan in the astrological horoscope. This is the esoteric use of the birth chart. However, before we discuss the mechanism of the horoscope, we must understand what it actually is. The natal chart is the schematic picture of the sky at the moment of birth at the point, in parallel, when the fine powder ceases to vibrate and becomes a fixed pattern, except here it is the position of the Sun, Moon and planets in the Zodiac and their disposition around the mundane House system that makes up the configuration. This celestial photograph is the record of the physical situation in the sky at the first breath. It must be seen not as the cause of the life pattern but merely as a cosmic timepiece that has been stopped. Here the simile is useful yet further. A clock is not time. Neither are the hands nor the numbers on its face. They merely show, in physical form, an arrangement of patterns that represent the time of the day. Likewise the positions of the celestial bodies in the Zodiac merely indicate the state of the invisible and subtle cosmic situation at a given moment. While it is said that the physical luminaries and planets have an effect, they are only influential by the law of synchronicity, that is that all simultaneous events are related. In this case the planets are at a particular location where they will impart a specific influence. Like a camera lens the planets, luminaries and Zodiac focus a cosmic situation into an image which is then manifested into the physical World. In kabbalistic terms, the lowest World merely expresses, in matter and energy, the changing interplay of the subtle forces that are themselves impelled by the dynamics of the World of Creation. Thus at the moment of birth a particular set of spiritual and psychological circumstances are concretised into the body and physical situation into which that spirit-soul emerges at that moment. The law of synchronicity or simultaneous events provides a total set of carnal, subtle and cosmic patterns fused into one life. So it is that when we look at a horoscope we are not just seeing the state of the sky but the moment when the incarnated entity is projected into a world designed to receive and test its capability. While some people may regard their fates as excessively difficult, we must take a larger view than the usually small and totally sensual and personal outlook most of us hold. A person is much older than his body. His memory goes back before birth. He will continue to ponder after death the problems he had to solve and yet still has to resolve in the next life. This is the real importance of the individual natal horoscope.

8. The Horoscope

The horoscope, as the word implies, means a 'view of time', that is a picture of the conditions at a given moment. In astrology there are several kinds of horoscope. It can be one of a coming event, an event that has passed or what the celestial situation is now. There are horoscopes of places, events and people at their birth, crisis points and deaths. There are horoscopes to determine the right moment when to do something and horoscopes to find out when to refrain from doing anything. All, however, follow a general set of principles which we shall examine in this chapter.

A horoscope can be cast in several graphic forms, the two best known being the square and the circular formats. The square, used in the Middle Ages and Renaissance, has gone out of fashion in the West and the circular one is now the most common. The reason for this is that the circle is graphically closest in diagrammatic form to what is actually seen by the eye of the Earth, horizons and the heavens. However, even within this simple formula there are variations according to which Mundane House system is used. The most familiar is the Placidus method but this is more to do with fashion than accuracy. The Campanus, according to some mathematicians, is in fact the closest to what can actually be seen by an astrologer standing on the site of his chart at the crucial moment. The Equal House system is favoured by some. It is an abstracted view of the sky which, while having many attractions for convenience's sake, has many faults.

To be precise, all the Mundane House systems have their faults as the art of astrology, unlike the exact science of astronomy, is closer to the impressionist painting than the high resolution photograph. But as any perceptive viewer will know, the precise edged image is usually less accurate and shallower psychologically than the subtle and graded painting. Life and people are not clear-cut. This is the first consideration when drawing up a chart—the precision of this or that degree is important but not as relevant as the overall impression of patterns and relationships within the horoscope. Moreover, it is a well-known phenomenon amongst serious astrologers that the best interpreters of

THE HOROSCOPE 71

charts are not always the pedants of numerical accuracy but the intuitive and often careless chart drawers. The ideal is, of course, the mean between the two. This can only be obtained by conscious effort as against mechanical work or psychic gifts.

Working from the data of time, day, month, year and location, let us assume we have a chart before us. Now again, there are various ways of approaching a chart but in this case we are not interpreting so much as trying to understand the implication of the mechanism of a horoscope. Firstly we must recognise that we are looking at a picture of the Earth and sky. True, it is arranged in a schematic form but it is, nevertheless, what is seen when looking due south (in northern latitudes) from the spot where the horoscope's subject was, is or shall be at the time being examined. Thus we have the sensual level displayed in that the Ascendant is the eastern horizon, the Descendant the western, with the Midheaven above our heads and the Nadir below and behind us. Moreover, depending on the time of day, the Sun will be literally represented as being above or below the Ascendant-Descendant axis line and the other planets set out according to their physical positions of rising, culminating, setting and so on. Likewise, the Moon's position will be graphically shown in one of the quadrants that divide the circle into rising and falling above and below the horizon. All this sets out, on the imaginary calibration that astrology has superimposed upon the sky, the precise geometric relationship between the celestial bodies in the Zodiacal band above and below the ecliptic path of the Sun as it traverses an annual circle. Very elementary stuff but factors many astrologers are remarkably vague about.

Taking a second step, we have to appreciate that behind this physical World manifestation is the subtle World of Formations. Here we see why the term 'sidereal' or 'starry' level is used, remembering that to the ancient and medieval mind this meant the planetary level of existence. Some Traditions, as said, call this level the 'astral' which has exactly the same meaning. A more important point, however, is to perceive the fact that the physical is dependent on the subtle World of change and not the reverse, as the sensually-oriented believe. The movements within the galaxy, the Solar system and indeed upon the Earth are not self-generated. They originate from the laws and principles spoken of earlier. The galaxy rotates according to the nature of large masses, and stars are born out of the energy and matter of creation. Likewise, the planets are formed from principles and laws operating upon molecular materiality and thus a particular set of electromagnetic and gravitational relationships determine the exact position of the planets in the Solar system. They are a *result*, not a cause, and their situations, when drawn into the horoscope chart, merely indicate the juxtaposition of subtle or psychological conditions present at that time in relation to that place. Like the uniqueness of an instantaneous photograph, all the factors that make the mood of a time are unrepeatable because in the next moment everything has changed, the event, state or person has moved on, evolved a psychological degree further along its fate towards its destiny. This introduces the third level of Creation or Spirit into the horoscope.

The World of Creation, it will be remembered, is the cosmic factor in Existence. By this is meant the grand design of Existence as it unfolds the Will of God. This is the gradual descent of the creative impulse out of the perfect World of Divine Emanation to its most physical manifestation and back again in the impulse of evolution that brings the Universe and its inhabitants into the Divine Presence again. However, on return all the experience gained of that cosmic cycle will have transformed the naïve spirit into the knowing and the submissive soul into the co-operative. The World of Creation manifests time and this provides the motion of the subtle World and the orientation of the physical World. In terms of the horoscope, the state of Creation and the stage it has reached are only perceived by those with the longest sight and deepest vision. If we could see the motion of the Milky Way on the physical level we might glimpse the scale of Creation; but no one lifetime is sufficient to detect the basic shift of even the nearest stars except by very old records or powerful instrumental magnification. Thus a sensually-based man, when confronted by this level of existence, cannot begin to comprehend the great movements in the Universe. He only sees a vast stillness that overawes and frightens him into clinging on to the known patterns of Nature and his own tiny life and preoccupations. Even such terrestrial events as earthquakes are deliberately ignored in a self-imposed psychological sleep of not recognising planetary activity. The San Andreas Fault under California is a kind of impossible myth belonging to another world to most of its inhabitants. Indeed, it is of another World and it will be so until triggered into its disastrous earthquake by the tension of the Solar system action upon that part of the Earth. It is worth noting the word 'disaster' means also 'of the stars.'

Entering into finer detail, the World of Creation can be detected in the physical aspect of the horoscope in the factor of the Milky Way,

Figure 16 — HOROSCOPE
Any major event in human affairs will not happen until everything, including the cosmos, is in the right place. Here the astrologer takes note of the celestial situation, before advising any client. A war, for example, might be imminent if Mars is in Aries squared to Saturn in Capricorn, opposed by Uranus in Cancer. Some sort of popular uprising against the State would be expected. Very useful intelligence for any ruler. (Robert Fludd, 17th century).

Figure 17—ZODIAC
This band of symbols is not related to the constellations, although originally their configurations matched. Due to the movement of the equinoxes, they no longer correspond. The design of each sign was not based on the position of the stars but the effect each area had on Earth when it was traversed by the Sun, Moon and planets. The Zodiac is like a series of stained glass windows which determine which colour or influence comes in from the cosmos. An image, like the fish-tailed goat, relates to the Sun shifting from a descending mode to the opposite after the Winter festivities and the ambitious, patient and practical people born during the thirty days or degrees the Sun was in Capricorn. (Dürer, 16th century).

the constellations and individual stars. The Great Year of the precession of the Equinoxes, which generates the Age of Aquarius, indicates the Earth's response to the grand design which the galactic and stellar Worlds implement. Thus the Earth in the Solar system follows the giant cosmic impulse of evolution, so that creatures born in certain epochs relate to the current stage of the galaxy whose stellar emissions, at varying frequencies of wavelength, produce particular mutations in organic life on Earth. So it is that the delicately balanced metabolism of Nature responds to match the incoming celestial influence in a wide array of plant, animal and human beings, each species and type absorbing and converting a particular range of vibration. Thus, for example, one flower absorbs all the colours of the spectrum except one which it rejects in the form of its display colour, like the red of the rose. Likewise with the animal kingdom; each creature's organism absorbs a particular quality of total energy and expresses in its life the reflection of that quality until the last of its species can no longer convert or meet the cosmic requirement and so it becomes extinct. Man, the spearhead of physical evolution containing all the other kingdoms, is the most versatile of the terrestrial creatures. So it is that during our age the human race is rapidly extending over the Earth's surface and almost eliminating the less efficient levels of life. No doubt this aberration is part of man's education into conscience and responsibility as the husbandman of the Earth. The cosmic intention is clearly indicated in many Traditions, that the planet should become a terrestrial paradise. This would aid the Solar system, refine the Milky Way and help fulfill the purpose of the Universe.

The Zodiac is the band of signs through which the Sun passes when viewed from the Earth. However, to be more precise it is a celestial zone rather than a collection of constellations because the astrological Zodiac is related to the Earth-Sun partnership. Thus there is the difference between the astrological and the stellar, astronomical, Zodiac. The chief implementer and converter of the incoming galactic influx is the Sun and so its position is major as regards the Earth and therefore the horoscope. This is because the Sun, as the nearest stellar body to the Earth, is the pivot of the Solar system and is composed of a level of energy and matter mid-way between the galaxy and the planets. As such it is the focus of galactic influence in the form of the Zodiacal principles which represent, in allegory, the twelve configurations of galactic energy and matter streaming in from the various surrounding zones of the Milky Way. Seen in analogue, the twelve signs can be regarded as twelve cosmic windows through which the galactic beams are refined and focused by the spheres of the planets and the lens of the Sun into the substance of the Earth.

Viewed from the standpoint of the horoscope of a person, the Sun position in the Zodiac defines the spiritual type of the being incarnated. Thus all Scorpios share the quality of that sign in their inner nature, that is the characteristics of the Self which is the essence of that person. This suggests that a subject of Scorpio (or any other sign) therefore cannot be an individual. This statement has a degree of truth in it. It is with great difficulty that our ego-Moon minds accept this notion but a little deep observation of members of our own Sun sign shows it irritatingly to be true. The Virgo is always preoccupied with detail and the Aries can never reject a challenge, nor can the Capricorn resist organising and so on. The fact is that each sign in a human being is an expression of the Creative World, the spiritual level of Existence, which is a simpler but more potent factor than either the subtle psychological or complex physical composition of a human being. However, each spiritual entity is given its particular individuality by the degree in the sign and the decan or three-split division of its sign. Thus, those with Sun in, say, twenty-three degrees of Leo or the third decan, sub-ruled by Mars, tend to be a militant Leo rather than the more merciful fifteen degrees Leo whose decan is sub-ruled by Jupiter. The modification and individualisation is carried further by all the rest of the chart which colours in and overlays the spiritual nature of the Sun by the planetary effects upon the balance of the psyche and the Lunar and Ascendant influence upon the body.

Needless to say, the various elements and angles have a bearing on the manifestation of the Spirit-Sun-Self complex. If the person's sign be, say, Taurus then the Self will manifest in a Fixed and Earthy manner, that is practical and inclined to be comfort loving, as against the Piscean who would express his Self in a Watery and changeable way in his sensitive but unstable response to life. At a similar level of being the active and passive aspects of the signs will show in, for instance, the active hustling of the Libra as opposed to the reflective formulating of the Capricorn. Here also begins the interaction of the signs with the Cardinal intriguing of the Watery Cancer upset by the Fiery, open initiative of the Cardinal Aries. Likewise is the confrontation or co-operation of opposites as happens between, say, the Fixed signs of the democratic Aquarius and the royal will of Leo. Ironically, as in all these opposites, each contains at its roots the opposing or complementary sign. Thus the vague but wise Sagittarius deep in Gemini drives the twins to seek in the collection of facts that which they cannot remember long enough to become wise, while the basically warrior sign of Aries deep inside Libra prompts the Libran to pursue diplomacy as a substitute for war. All the signs contain these opposites as each man contains a female principle and *vice versa*.

The Sun principle for each person is his or her connection with the World of the Spirit. As inner representative of the stellar level in the Solar system, the spiritual Sun is sometimes called the radiant body of a human being. When seen on the kabbalistic Ladder of four Worlds, the Sun can be observed to be the meeting place of the three lower Worlds and, as such, it performs as the junctional focus of the physical body's highest experience, the psyche's central seat of control and the spirit's bottommost connection to the incarnated soul and flesh. Astrologically speaking, the Sun-Self is the purest factor of the being in most people. It, like the physical Sun, radiates out that which is within its nature and absorbs that which is coming from the World above and the World below. If the Sun of a person is obscured by, say, the ego-Moon from below, or holds only to the spirit and cosmic levels above, there can be no flow of experience, no growth and no evolution. This is why the Sun sign is the most important in the horoscope. However, it cannot relate directly to the Earth below. Fate has to work through the planets that affect the person's life through the astral body. Thus the composition of the horoscope indicates not only the essential character but also the fate of that person which is but one life link in the long chain of his spiritual existence or destiny.

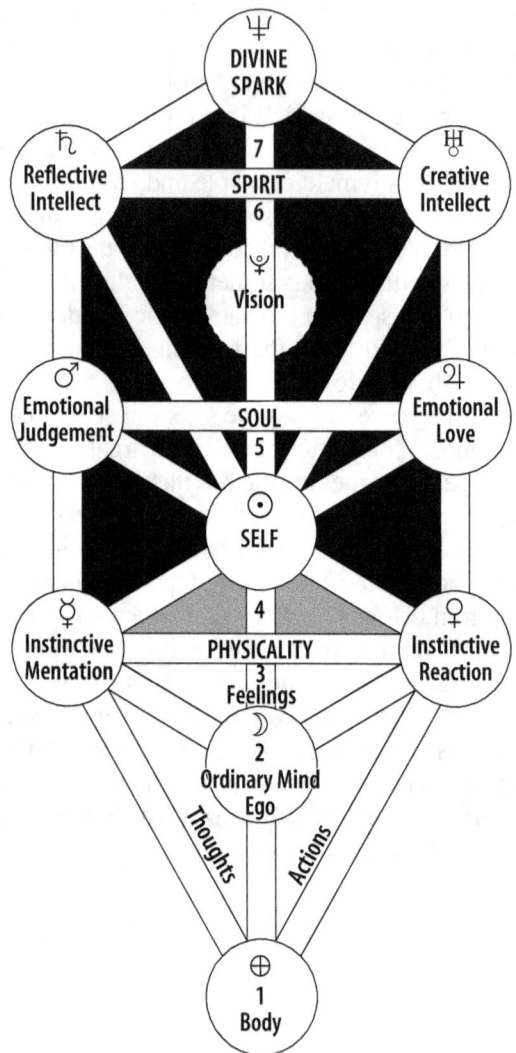

Figure 18—BASIC PSYCHE
In this Tree, the everyday mind centres on the ego, ruled by the Moon, while the surrounding triads define habit and conditioning. The triad made up of Sun, Venus and Mercury is the fourth mode of consciousness when we are particularly alert. The rest of the diagram is unconscious in most people. In this zone the psychological principles, symbolised by the planets, are at work but unnoticed except in dreams, irrational attitudes and compulsive actions that underlie and sometimes overrule conditioning. Pluto and Neptune are agents of the mystical experience people have perhaps once or twice in a lifetime. (Halevi).

9. *Planetary Emphasis of Psyche*

As the Sun in the horoscope is the linchpin, the place of interconnection between the Spirit and the physical body, so the planets in the chart represent the principles that make up the mediating psyche between them. The psyche belongs to the subtle World of reality. This means that its composition is more subject to variation than the purer level of the essential spirit and the very fixed and limited set of physical laws that govern the carnal body. Thus while all Sun Pisces, for example, are very alike in principle, as are all the signs to their types and all incarnate people have much the same model for a body, the degree of variety in the psychological spectrum is enormous, ranging from the imbecile to the genius, from the saint to the criminal and from the madman to the mystic. How and why is this so? The planetary level in a horoscope reveals just this.

Treating the planets according to the kabbalistic scheme one can, it will be remembered, divide them as pairs roughly into Mercury and Venus as the psycho-biological, Mars and Jupiter as the emotional and Saturn and Uranus as the intellectual pairs with Neptune and Pluto, the most remote couple, being the deepest inner connections, along with the Sun, to the cosmic level of the Spirit. Some would call these two the 'planets of transformation' as against the other planets of function that are placed upon the active and passive pillars of the psychological Tree. Viewed in this way, the blend of a planet in a particular sign takes on a wide significance. Let us examine some examples.

Supposing a chart has Uranus in Capricorn and Saturn in Aries. This would mean that the active side of the intellect, or the Uranian principle of revelation, would be contained by periodic Capricornian reflection. Thus new and original ideas arising from deep within the unconscious would have a philosophical flavour, rather like Sir Isaac Newton's moment of enlightenment when he saw the apple fall from a tree and perceived how the laws of gravity drew it to the Earth. The position of Saturn, the passive side of the intellect in Aries, would have the reverse effect. Aries, being an active sign, would stimulate some original reasoning but it would have a different quality from Uranus in Capricorn. It would, moreover, being square in aspect to Saturn's own sign of Capricorn, be under strain so that a certain illogicality would enter into the sequential reasoning and bring about some unusual quantum-jump thinking. However, while it could be, in one person, a clear foundation of a remarkable train of thought, in another it might be the raving of an irrational pedant. This loading would depend on other factors in the chart such as the Mercurial aspects and the placing in the mundane Houses of Saturn and Venus.

The positions of the planets Mars and Jupiter likewise modify their effects so that, for example, if Mars is in Libra, the emotional capacity of the person to be decisive is split. This problem is reversed if Mars is in Aries, its own sign, which can, if badly aspected, create an over-decisive emotional response. Here it must be repeated that Mars is not the principle of violence or passion but mainly of emotional control. The degenerate or negating aspects of this emotional principle only occur when the Martial constraint is confused, divided or over-reactive. Many religious zealots have an afflicted Mars which makes for self-righteous anger. Indeed the seven deadly sins, when placed upon the seven lower celestial principles on the Tree, reveal the negative side of their qualities. In the case of Mars it is obviously unjustified anger, with Jupiter it is envy. The reason for the latter sin is that Jupiter normally represents the merciful and generous aspect of a person's emotional life. When placed, for example, in Virgo it can make the person mean and niggardly. The sin is further compounded if Jupiter is badly aspected and if the man chooses to allow this flaw to dominate the psyche. Here enters the issue of free will which is exercised with particular cruciality between these two emotional planets. It can be said that Mars, the Sun and Jupiter form the triad of conscience. In Kabbalah this triad on the Tree is the place of the individual soul which is not only emotional by nature but, like the Sun, hung between the spiritual macrocosm of the unconscious and the ego-centric consciousness of the microcosmic body of the individual.

Venus and Mercury, for astronomical reasons, cannot be far removed from the Sun and so sometimes they are so close that they are what is called 'combusted' or blinded by its proximity. This means that the bio-psychological faculties that they represent sometimes cannot function fully and the person seems to be out of touch with the ordinary world about him—because both these planets are responsible for the input and output of psychological and physical information and action. Their position in the signs is critical in a person's performance and connection between his inner and outer Worlds. They are the first bridge or barrier. Thus Venus in its own sign of Taurus will be exceedingly sensual and creative while in Aries its detrimental placing will render its sensual activity to either self-censuring Puritanism or fierce over-indulgence. Venus's deadly sin is lust. Likewise with Mercury, if placed in the Watery Pisces, renders its precision into a slushy smear, as against a hyper-obsession for data when the planet is found in Gemini. Mercury's deadly sin is sloth.

All the above demonstrates how there are at least twelve possibilities for each of the six fundamental planets. These are again modified by whether they are in positive or negative signs, whether they are under a Fixed, Mutable or Cardinal influence or whether they are exalted, strong or in their detriment or fall, as well as the fine tuning of the first, second or third decan of the sign. This layering upon layering gives every psyche a particular balance and thus there is, without even taking the mutual aspects into consideration, a unique psychological composition in everyone.

The influence of Neptune and Pluto in the psyche is of quite a different order. Being the most remote, deepest and slowest of the planets, their placing in the Zodiac has the effect of a gradual and profound influence over the lifespan. Moreover as neither is, according to kabbalistic speculation, active or passive, their function is to pass on the more rarefied cosmic influxes from above or be receptive to the spiritual level present in the Worlds below. The zodiacal position of either of these two planets would be seen in the spiritual mood of a particular generation. For example, many of the people interested in things of the occult, the esoteric or mysticism were born after 1956 when Neptune entered Scorpio, the sign of occult matters. Only a few of the millions of people born prior to this date are interested in such matters and this is usually because their particular chart has this emphasis in it. There has not been such an interest by the young in unconventional religion for many years, if not decades. Neptune has a 164-year cycle which brings its past position in Scorpio in the mid-eighteenth century when the religious revival movements among the masses were being led, for example, by the Methodists in Britain for the Christians and by the similar popular movement of the *Hasidim* among the Jews of Eastern Europe. This is the cosmic effect of the planet. Pluto has a similar effect but it has not been observed long enough (it was only discovered in 1930) to ascertain its effects

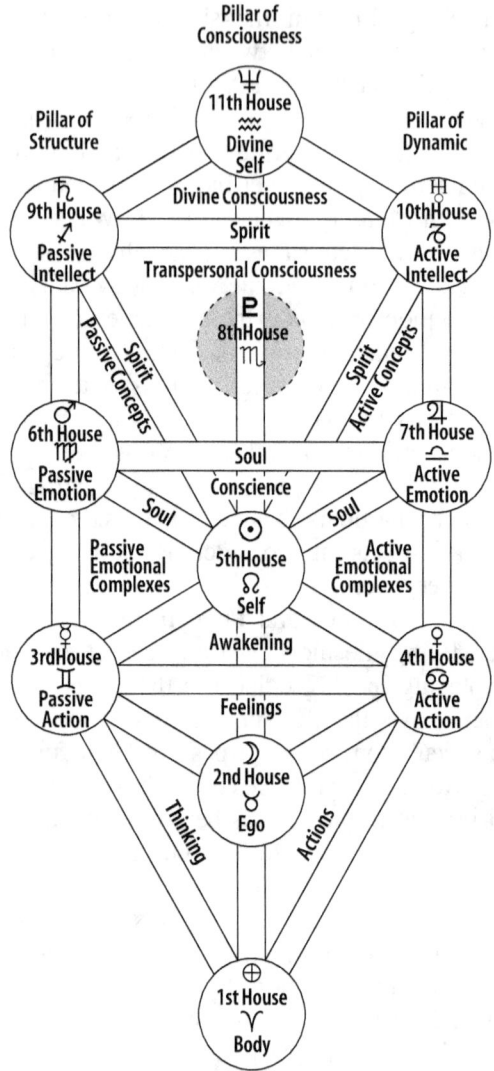

Figure 19—TREE CHART
Here, for the sake of clarity, the Zodiac cycle has been used to illustrate how each sefirah can be influenced by the sign in which it is placed. For example, the Moon in Taurus will produce an ego that likes comfort and, being in the second House, loves beautiful possessions; while Mars in Virgo would create a very critical faculty of Judgement, especially in matters of health. These and the other positions of sign and House would affect the triads, for example, of the emotional complexes. The Mars would make a person emotionally very discriminating and disciplined while Mercury would given them a sharp, intelligent wit. (Halevi).

precisely. All that can be said is that, as the most remote and slowest of planets, Pluto's function must be to transform the most broad scatter of cosmic influence before it enters the macrocosmic external and microcosmic internal Solar system of our incarnate World.

The mutual aspects of the planets, one to another, create both flows and resistances within the balance of the psychological anatomy. These aspects are based upon the geometric relationship of the celestial bodies within the context of the 360-degree circle of the horoscope. They describe the particular emphasis between this or that psychological principle. In some cases the angle produces a strong effect, in another a middle effect and in another a weak effect. Generally speaking the effects of the aspects are divided into good and bad. This is misleading. For example, Saturn and Mars are usually considered as malefics. Here is a misunderstanding of the real nature of the negative and positive side of cosmic principles. Again, take the so-called benefics of Venus and Jupiter. Because they appear to bring good fortune they are regarded as favourable; but consider the rich man's over-spoilt son or the woman with many lovers. Neither is usually happy, the first because he is never satisfied and is inevitably weak and the second because she never finds fulfilment in love and so wanders from lover to lover without relating to any of them.

In contrast, the severe lessons of Saturn and the astringency of Mars may seem, to the recipient of their apparent ill fortune, as tough but, nevertheless, their teaching incvitably, if taken intelligently, adds to the stature of the person and protects them from the shock of events that often destroy the frail ease of Jupiter's son and the shallow pleasure of Venus's daughter. It is likewise with the aspects. The trine and sextile are configurations of easy flow but in excess they can be the source of trouble. The grand trine may bring remarkable luck but it breeds laziness and lack of resilience. In contrast, the square and opposition may seem difficult but viewed from the standpoint of spiritual growth they become the benefactors in their challenge. The square can be turned into a two-pronged virtue and the opposition an axis of immense power. Even the grand cross or T-square can be reversed from an apparent crucial difficulty to a major advantage. Many people of great achievement have the cross, square and opposition. These aspects have given them tenacity while often those of considerable gifts granted by an excess of trines and sextiles have wasted their lives in a lack of effort and challenge to develop themselves to the full.

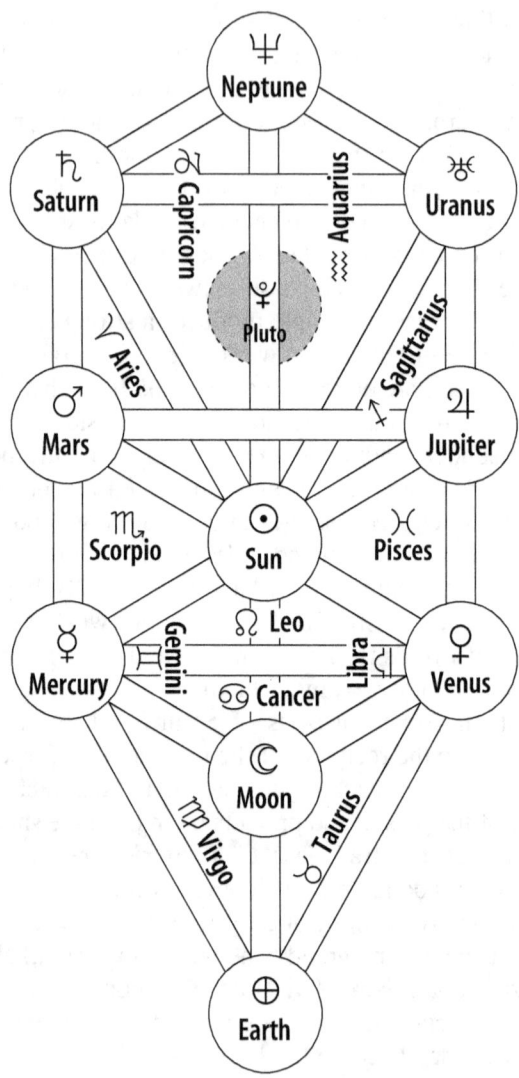

Figure 20—TRIADS
Each triad is related to a zodiacal sign. Venus, for example, rules Libra and Taurus, giving its triads a Venusian flavour, while Jupiter gives the active triads of emotion and concepts an expansive capability. This makes them open and idealistic but in danger of being overwhelming if not checked. The Leo and Cancer triads relate to the Self and ego, or major and minor levels of consciousness. The triads of Mars, Jupiter and the Sun relate to the soul while that of the Sun, Saturn and Uranus form that of the spirit; with Neptune, Saturn and Uranus making up the triad of the Divine in the psyche. (Halevi).

Seen as a whole, the aspects reveal the particular psychological set of planet-Zodiac configuration. Thus, for example, Venus square Mars indicates that the instinctive desires will sometimes press upon the emotional judgement and produce indiscrimination unless, of course, the tendency is consciously reversed and creates a remarkable sensitivity. Again, supposing Saturn is trine to the Sun. This will give the Self the ability to reason and follow through a sequence based upon a moment of truth. In negative it can produce a glib philosophy filled with over-simple rules. In the case of Jupiter square, say, to Neptune there will be a deep religious need that formal worship will not fill while with, say, Uranus trine Mercury there will be an unending flow of brilliant but erratic ideas and inventions. Every chart has a particular set of aspects and many astrologers call the patterns by such names as the Bucket or Splay, See-saw or Bundle. These names give at a glance the general configuration of the aspects and indicate the concentration or diffusion of forces in the psyche. The See-saw, for example, reveals a polarised nature, as against what is known as a Locomotive pattern which, like a nearly-complete wheel, makes for an almost all-round psychology. The advantages and disadvantages are power under limited focus as against wide but thinly spread talents. Both extremes and their in-betweens have their possibilities and problems. Objectively, everybody has exactly the same quota of strength and weakness. No-one, in the eye of God, has any advantage above or disadvantage below another.

The Moon in the psyche's anatomy is the ego. As such it acts as the intermediary between the physical and subtle Worlds. Its placing in the Zodiac determines the flavour of that particular ego. Thus the Virgo Moon will treat its education as a detailed programme of study while the Moon Cancer will simply absorb intuitively all the sights, sounds and general impressions about it so as to form an image of its home, culture and attitudes. The Moon Aries, on the other hand, will explore and take up the honest direct approach in contradistinction to the prudent, circumspect Capricorn Moon. All these ego flavours are developed during the early years of life and overlie all the planetary and Sun principles in the psyche. The effect is that, to the unperceptive, the Moon seems to be the psychological personality as against the physical type of the Ascendant. Personality comes from the root word 'persona,' or mask, and this is exactly what the Moon is, except that it is the vehicle by which we negotiate inwardly with our own subconscious and outwardly with others in social intercourse. For most people the ego-Moon is their psychology because their Self or Sun is not sufficiently developed to overcome the imprint of their upbringing. Indeed, Moon-dominated people are rigidly held within their social zone where the class's conventions and rules are almost absolute. Conformity is a Lunar quality that frequently eclipses the light of the Sun of the Self. The deadly sin of the Moon is avarice.

The Moon is the dully reflecting bio-psychological mirror, focused and patterned according to the sign it occupied at birth and overlaid by education and environment in early life. The particular flavour of its receptivity to the surroundings is affected by the planetary and Solar aspects to the zodiacal position, so that the ego can be subject to the eases and pressures of the intellectual planetary principles of Saturn and Uranus and the emotional factors of Mars and Jupiter. The placing of Mercury and Venus is, in one sense, even more influential because, as the inferior planets, they have a direct connection with the Moon-ego. Thus an afflicting Mercury will make the ego's mental processes race or be retarded while a well-placed Venus will give the ego a light charm and grace not to be expected in, say, a usually serious Moon Capricorn. The planets of Pluto and Neptune will not, unless strongly and very precisely aspected to the Moon, be perceived in any obvious way. But, for example, if Pluto were conjunct the Moon there would be present a strangeness in the personality that would disturb the possessor and intrigue the outside viewer. The psychological effect of Neptune in exactly the same position would give the ego an increased psychic ability and make the person fascinated by the unusual although, unless this was strengthened by other aspects, it might not be any more than a superstitious appreciation. As will be realised, the Moon-ego is not an originating principle. It only puts out and reflects what has been absorbed. However, its power is the bond of habit, in that the Lunar principle is concerned with maintaining rhythms, images and patterns. That is why the first or Lunar half of a life is crucial because it sets the model for most people's lives before they enter the last half of their life which is regarded as the Solar period.

Seen as a whole, the Moon is the lower focus or ego-consciousness of the psyche with the Sun as the upper or inner and, for most people, the unconscious focus of the psyche. These two luminaries are the axis of Will to the active and passive rôles of the six functional planets of Mercury, Venus, Mars, Jupiter, Saturn and Uranus. As such the Moon is the lower receptor of practically everything coming in from the outer world and the implementer of most things emerging from the unconscious. Because of the immediacy of the ego-Moon's consciousness, it and the person possessing it often believe that its identity and sensibility is the real 'them.' This is reinforced by the outside world which casts their ego-Moon into a distinct and recognisable image which the person gladly accepts or fiercely rejects—which indicates its power. This image, or the desire to have a recognisable identity, gives the ego-Moon a strong sense of its own importance. Its zodiacal position, plus the planetary and Solar aspects, play a very important part in the balancing and emphasis of the ego's image of itself. All the foregoing sets out the planetary body and its strengths and weaknesses. This is, of course, crucially affected by its placing in the mundane House system of the natal horoscope. The unique juxtaposition of the zodiacal configuration with the mundane system generates the potential fate of that individual, should they choose to come out of the domination of the Moon and under the guidance of their Sun.

10. The Houses and the Ages of Man

While the Zodiac, luminary and planetary principles and their aspects represent the particular configuration of the psyche, the relationship between these subtle arrangements and the mundane Houses indicates how the incarnating entity will manifest in the Natural World. Developed over many centuries, the mundane House system is a scheme based upon zodiacal principles which acts as a static overlay upon the ever-moving sky. Thus, taking the classic pattern which is modelled on the year but in reverse, the noon position or 10th and 9th Houses are occupied by the Winter signs of Capricorn and Sagittarius with the zenith position corresponding to the Winter Solstice. The nadir opposite at the base of the system is between the 3rd and 4th Houses which are related to Gemini and Cancer, with the Summer Solstice between. At a left angle on the Ascendant comes the dawn of the day whose 1st House is based upon Aries, the Spring Equinox sign. Likewise, opposite, the Descendant is related to the Autumn Equinox with the 7th and 6th Houses echoing Libra and Virgo. The reason for the reversal is not only that the apparent daily motion of the sky and the true yearly movement of the Sun and planets are counter to each other but also that the mundane scheme is a mirror image of the celestial situation.

In essence, the mundane House system is a sector pattern pivoted upon the place where the birth or event was, is or will occur. Through its radiating windows the Zodiac and its contents may be seen in relation to the horizon of the site. From the placing of the signs and celestial bodies can be ascertained how the person—if it is a natal chart—will express his psyche. Taking the ego first, let our example be Moon in Virgo in the 10th House. This house, according to Tradition, is concerned with achievement in the world because it is based upon the ambitious sign of Capricorn and is at the height of the daily cycle. The 10th House is the *practical* zenith while the 9th is the *ideal* zenith because it is based on Sagittarius. Moon in Virgo in the 10th, therefore, will tend the ego of the person towards a double Earth application of his acquired personality in matters of organisation, administration and

Figure 21—HOUSES
This old print defines the function of the static twelve House divisions of the sky in a birth chart. The image of a king in the 10th House denotes worldly achievement while that of Death in the 8th represents karma or that which was brought in from the last life. The Houses are related to the Zodiac but refer, according to what is in them, to how the chart will manifest in the everyday world. For example, if the Moon is in the 3rd House of the Twins, the ego mind-set will be lively, talkative and curious about everything while Venus in the 3rd might make poetry or singing part of that individual's talent. (16th century woodcut).

all those professions associated with the blend of Virgo and Capricorn, such as hospital administration, publishing, big business, accounting, National Health Service and so on. The person, if the aspects to the Moon are good, will slowly rise to become a prominent administrator with a reputation for scrupulous thoroughness and detail, although sometimes inclined to be caught up with some small items that attract his attention as unjust or careless. Moon in Leo in the same House would manifest the ego in quite a different way. Here the ego would lack the modesty of the Moon Virgo and insist upon a recognition that it might not merit. Indeed a touch of megalomania, but with style, might make a charismatic personality but, unless well aspected, the driving 10th House ambition to be a popular Leonine figure might cause some suffering and continuing humiliation. Here we see how the interaction between the interior nature and the outer world begins to produce a particular life or fate.

The positions of the planets in the signs and in the mundane Houses create a wide variety of manifestations. For example, Mars in Virgo in the 7th House of Partners would make the person highly choosy about his companions and any relationship, be it professional or private, would be made difficult by the constant detailed judgement and criticism going from one side to the other, for like would attract like response. Because of this, the type of partner the person would take in marriage, for example, would be narrowed down to a very fastidious spouse with certain looks, manners and emotional expectations. Unless there was some other mitigating factor like Venus in Aquarius in the 5th House, the person would never ever become involved with an ill-mannered, sloppily dressed and over-emotional lover. In contrast, if Mars were in Pisces in the 7th House, this would create an emotional indecisiveness that would result in a constant reversal of the emotional balance in any relationship, making the dominant aggressor suddenly turn into the confused victim. This could clearly affect the kind of marriage the person might attract to himself.

Here we observe again the law in that we, by our natures, make for ourselves our particular kind of life. Thus two people born in the same home, with the same education, will live out entirely different lives because of the way in which their particular psyche manifests and generates its own fate. For a classic example, supposing a pair of twins are born but there is, as often is, a few minutes' difference. This can be crucial, as the Zodiac moves a degree every four minutes. It can mean that Saturn in Scorpio is in the 8th House of the elder twin and in the 7th of the younger. Out of such a difference can be generated a deep interest in the occult philosophies in the former and a profound attraction to older members of the opposite sex in the latter. Clearly the two lives can take quite different directions if the Saturn is particularly well- or ill-aspected. The former might well pursue a lifetime of secret inquiry into spiritual evolution while his brother is preoccupied with working out his relationship with his mother through a grim marriage to an older woman. Obviously, the greater the gap between the twins the more the whole Zodiac rotates within the mundane House system and thus the less like each other the twins will appear. This is without taking into account the Moon's rapid movement in the course of, say, two hours when it can just cross from one sign into another by a degree. The example of the twins born on the same day at different times illustrates well how almost identical subtle natures can produce quite different lives.

As may be inferred from the above, the planets in the signs set within the Houses reveal how and where the various intellectual, emotional and practical aspects of the nature will express themselves in a terrestrial situation. The same is true of the Sun. However the difference here is that the Sun holds a special position in that it is the pivot of the being incarnated. As such it will, if its full power is developed, make the person's fate truly individual. By this is meant that instead of living off the socially-educated ego-Moon, as most people do, the person operates according to his essential Solar nature. The Solar mark of such people is often seen in the great explorers, painters, thinkers, soldiers, poets and scientists. These people follow their star which, in fact, means their Sun. Now for obvious reasons the position of the Sun in a sign and within a House is very critical in how this individuality shows itself. For example William Blake, the mystical poet, had Sun in Sagittarius, the metaphysical sign, in the 5th House, the place of creativity and fame. He also had Jupiter and Mercury there, so that he had the emotional power and articulation to express his vision.

In contrast Oliver Cromwell, the stern but deeply religious Lord Protector of England, had the Sun in the Fixed sign of Taurus in the 1st House with Aries in the Ascendant. This gave him a practical directness and yet, with Moon in Virgo in the 6th House, an eye for detail and subtlety. He was the only military dictator England has had. King Henry VIII, of multiple marriage fame, had Sun in Cancer in the 10th House. This gave him the power to unify the English nation after

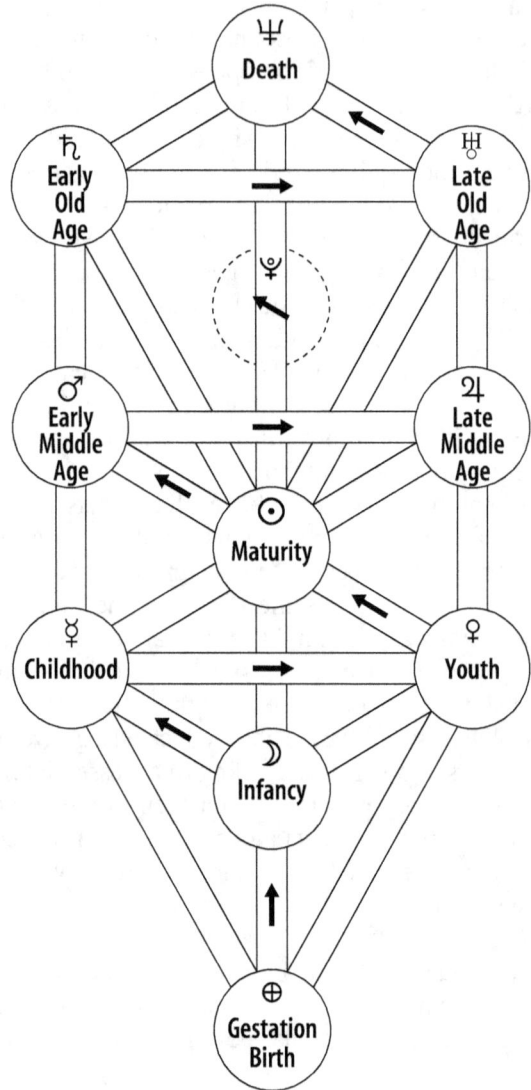

Figure 22—AGES
Between birth and death there are clearly recognisable stages, each related to a sefirah and celestial body. They last approximately seven years. What is not always observed is that while a person may grow older in body, their mind may fixate at the Lunar, Mercurial or Venusian stages. Many middle-aged people are still quite infantile or childish. In the process of inner development, one must reach Solar maturity before going on to Martial discipline, Jovial openness and the higher aspects of evolution, symbolised by the superior planets. (Halevi).

a long period of civil war and, with Moon in Aries in the 7th, time to become impulsively intoxicated, then bored, with several wives. His Sun and Moon were squared.

Gladstone, the grand old man of Victorian politics, had Sun in Capricorn in the 1st House with Mercury in conjunction and thirteen degrees of Capricorn on the Ascendant. He outlived most of his contemporaries and was famous for his ponderous verbosities. True to Capricorn legend, he was still asked to be Prime Minister in his mid-eighties. While the foregoing examples illustrate only the famous on record, it must be noted that the same principle of the combination of the Sun sign and House applies to all charts. The Sun is the principle of the fulfilment of the fate. It is the prime of a person's life and, incidentally, subject to its deadly temptation, pride. To understand this we must return to the moment of birth and follow the progression of fate through its general phases of life.

Tradition says that there are seven planetary ages of man. The first is under the Moon. This can be said to cover the period from conception—which is clearly concerned, in a woman's ovulation cycle, with a Lunar principle—to the end of babyhood. Here the Moon quality of the baby, virtually orbiting the mother and sucking the fluids of her Earth body, are plainly seen. So is the ebb and flow of sleeping and waking, eating and excreting and the Lunar-like changes of mood as the small smooth watery being slowly grows in the post-gestation vegetable period of its life. At this point it is well to think about the word 'being' because the whole process of life is the 'coming to be.' From this first stage which supplies the physical vehicle, the person incarnated passes on to the age of Mercury.

Here childhood begins as the life maintenance systems, now stabilised, are superseded by the shift of attention to the development of the Mercurial intelligence that the animal part of man acquires to look outward. In this stage the child takes to escaping periodically from its orbit round the mother in excursions of curiosity, the hallmark of Mercury. It performs all sorts of experiments like weighing, throwing, dipping in water, playing with fire in order to find out about the world. As it grows into full childhood it collects things, enjoys games, asks endless questions and continually pries into everything strange and peculiar—another quality of Mercury.

With the advent of adolescence comes the age of Venus with its strong likes and dislikes, preoccupation with attraction and repulsion, pleasure and pain, love and violence. Venus is not the goddess of love but of passion. She is only interested in what satisfies her and if it does not she rejects and sometimes destroys the now-hated objects of her passion. The Venusian feelings and preoccupations last up till the late twenties in most people and, needless to say, this is the period when many people mate, thus completing the vegetable and animal parts in themselves and procreating the next generation. From this time on a new period begins as the life moves out of the biological into the psychological phase—if there is the desire to evolve.

The Sun period is the next stage. This begins as the person attains the physical peak of the body's capacity at around thirty. By this time, a person has experienced enough of life to assess his physical and psychological gifts, capabilities and limitations. It is the truly Solar period when the truth about one's nature begins to dawn. Up till this point all has been possibility. The art student realises that her talent is in fact not of a major painter but a minor gift which has found its true level in designing book jackets. The brilliant schoolboy inventor discovers that he is not actually original but is very clever at solving mechanical problems in an engineering company. The natural leader of the village football team has found that he has a gift for running a large farm while a troubled, introvert nurse finds herself specialising with maladjusted children.

By the time the Sun age is entered upon, the quality of the particular life is possible to perceive, if not by the person himself, then certainly by his friends and colleagues. A man may try to live upon his ego-Moon image but his associates know exactly what he can and cannot do. While one man, despite his Moon's boasting, never gets promotion another who is naturally modest is always being offered better assignments as his Solar capability is recognised and his reputation grows. The Sun level is the beginning of the next stage of development of being because it is from the Sun that the real task of a person's life stems. This is why the position in the sign and House of the Sun is so crucial in a chart. If a person has, suppose, his Sun in Gemini in the 10th House he may well reach his place as a famous journalist or scholar of renown by thirty. Likewise here will be the life's task, to bring the factor of truth and integrity to a popular or learnèd audience. In this will be a full way of life and the beginning of the actualisation of his potential fate.

The period of Mars is that of early middle age. It is when the physical and psychological capacity is at its maximum and the direction of the life is strongly focused. Thus the architect who has established

Figure 23 — LEVELS
A person may have a very favourable birth chart. However, this may make him lazy. This can lead him to remain at the mineral level of not making any effort. Likewise, he can stop at the vegetable stage, content with his lot. Animal people at least make the most of their fate, if only to prove themselves. People seeking to be truly human often have difficult horoscopes as challenges to develop their weaknesses and to clear karma. (Woodcut, 16th century).

himself during the period from around thirty to forty begins to be recognised as having a definite approach. Here is the discipline of Mars sharpening the aim of the life. It is often a controversial epoch as he is a force to be reckoned with by his competitive peers and those holding the dominant places in the profession. He will make enemies and have to fight for what he stands for. This he can now do with all the Martial skill at his command, based upon experience and an established reputation. He will have to make decisions now upon which people's lives and jobs depend. No one will question his capability if he has fought well. Only the difference of approach will be questioned.

In time he will pass into the Jupiter period associated with late middle age where he begins to soften, becomes less physically tough and he no longer has to defend his established kingdom or his actions. He will, from now on and with his acquired wealth of material and experience, be able to be generous practically and tolerant psychologically. He will become blander, more expansive although, if his Jupiter is in a constricting sign like Virgo, he will be bad-tempered and economic in his generosity. If life has treated him well, he will have compassion upon others. If not, then he will begin perhaps to forgive himself as he slips into a less strenuous phase of taking up the gracious king rather than the warrior rôle.

In time this epoch creeps into early old age, the period of Saturn which is the planet of reflection and understanding. In this phase he reviews his life and sees, positively or cynically, the effect of the world on himself and he upon the world. To most whose inner dreams of the ego remain, as they must, unfulfilled, the Saturn period is hard and sullen. Past times are seen in the long view and hindsight as patterns and cycles. Crossroads are perceived in retrospect and opportunities not recognised at the time are viewed in the rhythms of fate. Thus in this period the quality of the life is revealed to the person, the successes and failures assessed and acknowledged or denied this side of death.

In the Uranian period of late old age revelations can occur about the life lived. Finally, the Neptunian moment comes when the person experiences a flash of the Divine when they are disembodied. After this moment the post-mortem process begins, prior to rebirth..

All people follow this general planetary progression. However, what gives a particular fate its movement is not only the unfolding of the various ages but the continuing motions of the planets as they transit and aspect the configuration of the original natal chart. Here is where the details of fate can be predicted—but only to a certain degree. This is the study of astrological progressions.

Figure 24—WHEEL OF FORTUNE
This is not a random process or a regular cycle but a pattern in which a birth chart is activated or retarded by celestial conditions. Here Mars rules for a while before being replaced by the Sun. Below, the Moon and Mercury are in restrained positions. In kabbalistic and psychological terms, the sefirot and functions are stimulated or stymied, leading to bursts of action or frustration. (Medieval woodcut).

11. Unfolding Rhythms

The basis of fate is the initial setting of the subtle anatomy into the solid form of the carnal body and the progressive unfolding of this blended pattern throughout the subsequent life as the cosmic flow interacts with the individual's response to it. The moment of crystallisation at birth has been discussed in detail but a brief recapitulation might be helpful before we examine the effect of the progressions in a person's life.

The moment of conception takes place at the point of interaction between the spiritual, subtle and physical Worlds. Here the spirit of the entity, which operates on a totally different time scale from the Worlds below, initiates the process whereby the subtle body that enclothes it is connected, in the physical event of organic union, to a fertilised cell. Thus conception is never an accident but a carefully selected moment in time designed to fit into that being's particular needs for development and task. During the months of gestation when the physical vehicle is being constructed, the subtle body is still in its highly fluid state but its psychological viscosity is slowly stiffened as it becomes more and more enmeshed into the growing body in the mother's womb. Obviously there are times when, through choice, the pregnancy is aborted, either by the parents, the incarnating entity itself or Providence. This may happen because of the factor of free will on the human level (incarnate or discarnate) or because the abortion is a lesson in itself, as the birth might have been. If the pregnancy is to be completed then the moment for entry into the physical World is again carefully selected. As experience shows, few births occur on a medically fixed day. It is usually earlier or later than the theoretically expected time. This is due to the position of the Moon which has a profound influence on both the mother and the baby so that, as the lowest celestial factor, it governs the moment of birth as it did the period of conception in the mother's monthly menstruation cycle. Here again, one must remember the Moon and indeed all the other celestial bodies are only the physical expressions of subtle rhythms in a vast creative process.

At the moment of birth, when the first independent breath is taken, many switch processes take place in the baby's body to convert its metabolism from feeding off the mother via the placenta. Suddenly it comes out of a watery environment to breathe and live in a world of air. Abruptly it is no longer totally supported but has to survive semi-independently. The change that takes place is enormous, not only to the body but also to the psyche which now finds itself completely locked into a fleshy vehicle.

Some entities, it has been observed, are delighted to be incarnated and show it in a joyous cry, while some are angry and shout protest and some simply accept their incarnation and remain placid. It is said that this is the age of wisdom because the baby still remembers where it came from and what it has to pass through. This knowledge is, however, soon overlaid by the sheer weight of the physical toil that goes into living within a rapidly growing body of tissue. From our viewpoint, the important moment is the first breath because it is at this crucial instant that the subtle body gels and sets.

The first thing that precipitates the crystallisation is the Ascendant, or the Zodiacal sign the Eastern horizon is turning into. Out of this initial terrestrial and celestial interaction, where the sky makes its impact upon the Earth, comes a distinct print which is stamped upon the form or appearance of the body just born. Thus, if Taurus is rising the body will take on and develop the form of that sign and if, say, Mars is also present this will modify the Taurean ease and toughen and darken its visage. The rest of the chart, of course, will take on the qualities of the signs in the Houses and the interaction of the planets and luminaries. This means that the incarnated psyche is focused into a particular psychological matrix into which the body grows. Unlike the scientific view, astrology holds that the body conforms to the psyche and not the reverse. Thus a person slowly fills out, during his life, the already existing form that was crystallised at birth. The modifications of this form, of course, pass through their seven planetary ages but these are part of a general progression. The particulars of fate, however, are determined by the person's response to the unique gelling at the moment of birth, expressed graphically in the natal horoscope. Here starts the interaction of the static and dynamic aspects of fate.

Firstly, contained in the original natal moment are all the talents, strengths and weaknesses of the person. This is the point of departure. From the moment of birth onwards the processes of 'coming to be' continues in the natural world, each stage opening out, testing and developing through success and failure, rapid motion and long waiting, the being of the person. The synthesis of the fate is said to be in the 'Dragon's head and tail' which are the North and South nodal points of the Moon or the Lunar axis of rise and fall. These are also called the points of 'ease' and 'unease' and represent the chief areas of success and difficulty in a person's fate. The reason for this is that the Moon is the foundation of the person and therefore the nodes represent the extremes as realised in the psycho-physical interaction of that life. Thus, someone with his ascending Node in the 1st House and his descending Node, therefore, in the 7th will have no problem in presenting himself in public but his private life will be different. The reverse would be the case if the 'Dragon's head' were in the 7th. These patterns are set for life so as to develop the person as a whole. Here it must again be stated that like so-called bad aspects or planets, the apparent weaknesses or difficulties are areas to be worked on and converted into strengths.

There is no such thing as a disastrous chart. The setting of the chart then is the platform from which the now incarnate being begins his journey through earthly experience. From his birth he is given an interior pattern which will generate a particular life style in relation to the exterior world. During this lifetime, however, he has three choices: to develop, just maintain what he is or go down in quality of being until he is released by death from that chart's encapsulating form. Now, while the horoscope may be regarded by some as a confining prison, it is in fact a supporting pattern to guide and indicate one's gifts, faults and path through life. No one, not even the Messiah himself, can avoid the form of fate because even His life must be expressed through a psyche and a natural body. However, for lesser mortals the impetus comes not from the potent impulse of the creative spirit of destiny but from the push of events in the subtle World of the planets, their effect upon mankind in general and within the individual psyche in particular. These events are prompted by the phenomenon of progressive aspects as the heavenly processes move on after the moment of birth.

The first rhythm to be experienced is that of the Ascendant or the Earth's daily rotation. In this is sensed the peaks and troughs of physical performance. Often, for example, the person born with the Sun in the 1st House or at dawn finds that his best time of day is the early morning while another with Sun in the 10th finds that around noon is his most lucid and energetic hour. The effect of the daily rotation of the sky is, of course, affected by the luminary and planetary aspects to the Ascendant and midheaven but the general principle is that the twenty-four-hour cycle takes its trimming from the Ascendant. Thus, for example, someone with, say, Gemini on the Ascendant will be immediate in nervous response as against a slow gut reaction in a Cancerian Ascendant. These factors would only apply, however, to the bodily day-by-day rhythms which are considerably overlaid by the effect of the Moon as it runs its Lunar cycle.

The Moon has a twenty-eight-day cycle and so, in relation to the original Moon position in the chart it is, during this monthly cycle, passing through various aspectual relationships to the natal Moon. The effect is again principally bodily in as much as it will influence the balance of the body fluids and the speed of the metabolic rate. The example of blood coagulating at different speeds in relation to the Moon's phases illustrates the point, as do many other biological rhythms, great and small, which are geared to the daily and monthly timekeepers of terrestrial and Lunar clocks. The Moon, however, not only affects the body's states, making it sluggish when in square or tense when in opposition or conjunction to the natal Moon, but it influences the condition of the ego which, it will be recalled, is part physical and part psychological in construction. Thus, for example, when the Moon is in Capricorn and trined to the natal Moon in Virgo, the person becomes calmer and more able to relate the long view of Capricorn with the detailed outlook of the Virgo. A little observation over a month soon brings into the consciousness these bio-psychological changes that extend our daily sensual states into moods of elation or depression, clarity or confusion, well-being or off colour. The Lunar effects are not deep and pass as the Moon shifts a sign every two days. For most people this Lunar conditioning is their inner life and state. To the perceptive, however, there is a great deal more to be observed, beyond the ego-Moon, of the planetary effects upon the psyche.

The rhythms of Mercury and Venus are about three and six months respectively and their effect is also bio-psychological. However, unlike the Moon they do not have a simple zodiacal cycle but oscillate about the Sun, never going beyond one or two signs away. The result of this is that they have an apparently more erratic and local effect upon the mind and body as they swiftly shift and then backtrack in their passage round the Zodiac. An example of this would be Mercury in Pisces, where it has its fall and produces a general lack of precision and communication in worldly affairs. This would clear up for a time when the planet entered Aries but again blur and confuse a person when it retrograded back into Pisces. A similar situation would occur when Venus was, suppose, in Libra where it is most powerful. Such a position would have its worldwide effect of Venusian stimulus on fashion and the arts, for example, and in the case of the individual with, say, Moon in Libra the impact would make the person's ego enhanced both in Venusian desire and desirability, thereby prompting some notable sensual event or encounter. Generally speaking, the effect of these two inferior planets is less noticeable than that of the Moon and the other celestial bodies, because their impact is often lost between the body and ego's changing states and the underlay of the superior planets which create the moods of the unconscious levels. As the intermediaries between the body and the psyche, Mercury and Venus act as the passive receiving and the active imparting factors which, because of the set of aspects and positions in a chart, make a person particularly susceptible to this or that interior or exterior event in one season and the reverse in the next, like being very sociable every late Autumn but distinctly anti-social every early Spring. This is apart from the general affect they have on everyone when they pass through their own exaltations, strengths, detriments and falls.

The Sun's annual revolution is the most obvious of the cycles. Anyone with some sensitivity to the subtle World can detect his or her personal year as against the natural cycle of the seasons. For the Capricorn (in the northern latitudes) the physical winter is his psychological summer, as for the Libra the natural Spring is his dark time. Likewise, the Solar quarter of the subtle year for each person unfolds the essential mood of his life for that year, so that when he reviews the present at any time he can perceive, by noting whether the Sun is currently, say, in first trine or second square to his natal sign, whether he is in his psychological late Spring or mid-Autumn. This is a very useful piece of knowledge because it reveals the waxing or waning Solar vitality in relationship to the natal Sun and helps show when to move and when to refrain from moving. For example, it is not a good time for a Leo to begin an enterprise when the Sun is in Scorpio because he will meet hidden resistance, something with which the royal and open sign of Leo could never cope. It would be better to wait until the Sun had moved into Sagittarius where two Fire signs can combine at full power. As it happens, while most people are oblivious of these combinations, they nevertheless unconsciously apply experience as they find opportunities open up or close down during their personal yearly cycle. In essence, the passage of the Sun round the Zodiac to its annual return to its original natal position in the chart marks out the prime timekeeper of the fate. Against it we measure our progress and the greater and lesser rhythms of the superior and inferior planetary principles.

The first pair of the superior planets are Mars and Jupiter, or the passive and active emotional principles of the psyche. They have a two-year and twelve-year cycle respectively. This means that Mars takes about two months to pass through a sign while Jupiter spends about a year in each one. The effect of Mars in a sign, depending on whether it is well or badly favoured there, is to precipitate confrontation and decision at the emotional level. Thus when Mars passes through the 7th House of a person in the sign of Aquarius there will be many dramatic moments in which the spouse or business partners will be forced to reconsider the whole deal. In contrast, if the House of Partners contains Taurus, the judgement of what is correct may be blurred by the pleasures of the relationship so that a man or woman, for the sake of good food and bed, may lose the chance to dissolve an essentially non-developing relationship. The effect of Jupiter is different in that, when this planet is passing through, suppose, Sagittarius, one of its own signs, its impact will be to open up great professional possibilities for a person who has the sign in, say, his 10th House. In its opposite sign, Gemini, the expansion of Jupiter will be fragmented and its power scattered. Such an event, when placed in, say, the 5th House could result in some unexpected child or series of love affairs. This means that a person observing that Jupiter or Mars is about to transit a certain House or crucial natal position can expect a precise effect from the event. Herein lies the principle of prediction, based upon the current position of the planets.

The other superior planets generate the same causes and effects but each in their own way as they pass through the signs and aspect the natal Sun, Moon and other planets. Saturn and Uranus, the passive and active intellectual principles, have roughly a thirty and eighty-year cycle. Saturn's progress is quite easily recognisable when it moves through certain Houses, like the 1st and the 7th, because its severe teaching methods invariably give the person's relationships with others a grinding but thorough review that usually resolves into a new but long-term outlook upon the world and its inhabitants, especially those close by. Here we should mention the effects of the

Figure 25 — TRANSITS
The ever-changing relationships between the celestial bodies generates cosmic weather. This affects humanity in general and individuals who have charts that resonate with what is going on in the sky. If there is a strong Saturn configuration, then people who are particularly affected will feel dull and depressed if afflicted or steady and determined if favourably aspected. These episodes are designed to give time for reflection or take advantage of a Saturnine situation. (Woodcut, 16th century).

aspects of the planets as they move. For instance, as Saturn hovers in Cancer in the 4th House of Security, it will not only lean heavily on the domestic situation but will affect, by opposition, the profession in the 10th House and the squared Houses and signs of Aries in the 1st and Libra in the 7th. Saturn will, however, be trine to Scorpio and Pisces in the 8th and 12th Houses, giving rise to much reflection about the inner meaning of life. This would be a very critical period for anyone with a chart showing this set-up.

Uranus, having such a long cycle, only affects the signs once during most lifetimes. However, as it moves through the aspects of the natal chart it will trigger both outer crises and inner revelations. Thus as it moves through the Zodiac, away from its natal position, it comes into sextile, square and trine aspect, in the first half of the life, before coming into the major opposition to its original position at around forty. This usually precipitates the person's most important revelation when he sees, at the mid-point of his incarnation, the first good and bad fruits of his labours. The Uranus effect is often very dramatic because it is around the forties that, for example, the professional peak is reached and a marriage is considered a success or a failure. Everyone passes through the Uranus crisis and enters the second half of their lives with considerably greater wisdom if the lesson is learned. Uranus is the planet of revelation.

The outermost planets of Pluto and Neptune have, as we saw earlier, only a very general effect. But, in as much as we are sensitive, their influence can be faintly detected as they pass through the signs and the Houses of the chart. Firstly, for example, Neptune's place in Libra would give a strange flavour to a whole generation's attitude to marriage, on the large scale, while its position in the 7th House in an individual's chart would emphasise this view for the period it was there. The slow motion of Neptune and its creeping aspecting to everything else would produce a gradual mystification and demystification of the signs, planets or Houses it was aspecting. The same would be true of Pluto which moves at an even slower speed. Pluto's effect, however, would be even more difficult to define in that its influence would be almost an imperceptible change, through its aspects, of the emphasis of various factors in the individual horoscope. For instance, a man might only realise after many years that a period of Plutonian suffering was necessary medicine for his Sun conjunct Moon in Leo vanity.

From all that has been discussed, it can be seen that there is a multiplicity of ever-changing rhythms and aspectings. Out of these dynamics arises a changing mood of a time and, for the individual, the development of the kind of life that was present in potential at birth. For obvious reasons, the calculation of all combinations is not only immensely complex but almost impossible to analyse accurately enough to make a precise prediction, because such a subtle scheme for each life is beyond the ordinary capability of the astrologer who can err considerably by being out by just one factor. Therefore honest astrologers down the ages, while making short-term, detailed prognostications based upon the celestial positions currently observable, have devised various simple techniques of general long-term prediction such as the Solar progression. This we shall examine in the next chapter.

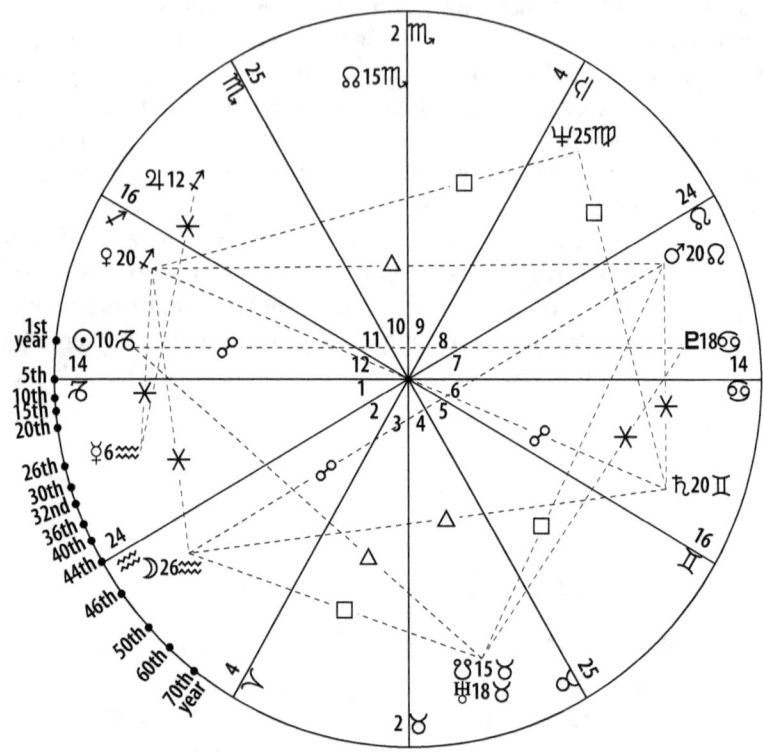

Figure 26 — PROGRESSION
Besides the normal movements within the Solar system, astrologers have discovered, over the centuries, that one day's cycle after birth corresponds to one year in later life. It reveals another dimension in fate. Thus in one case of this birth chart, around the age of forty-four when the Sun enters the House of Possessions, the person may find they come into some source of wealth. While this factor is background to every day, month and year, it can be considered as a crucial explanation, when nothing else is obvious, when fate seems unexpectedly cruel or kind. Life has many karmic levels. (Halevi).

12. *Prediction: A Sample Life*

Of all the various methods of prediction for seeing the general trends of a life, the Sun progression is probably the most common. This consists of saying that one degree equals one year, so that the Sun is moved in the tenth year, for example, ten degrees on from the original natal position. From the aspects radiating from this position some kind of assessment may be made about what is happening in that year of life. As might be expected these will only be outstanding events when there is a precise aspect, such as an exact square to Mars indicating a year of decision or the crossing of a House or sign cusp when the quality or emphasis of the life might change. The principle is very simple and because of this can only be seen in very wide terms or trends. Thus the type of events predicted have several possibilities for many reasons, one being, for example, that it is only the Sun that is involved. Another factor is that it depends upon the level of development of the person and yet another that a coincidental planetary configuration may be powerful enough to affect the progressed Solar inclination to do this or react that way. This is why prediction is not reliable. Besides there is always the element of choice which we will discuss later. But first let us look at a sample life from the progressed point of view to get the sense of the fatal pattern of life.

To begin with, the chart used as our example is a totally fictitious one. Moreover, it not only belongs to no one but it is not related to any known period. It is simply a device to get a maximum display of principles. Having said this, let us first build up a picture of the character of our fictitious person whom we shall call FP. With Sun in Capricorn in the 12th House one would expect him to grow into a reflective, hardworking, slightly formal retiring man. However, this is modified by Mercury in the 1st which indicates that he can be articulate and sociable, it being in Aquarius. Being unaspected by any major factor except a weak sextile to Jupiter, the Mercurial talk could be just a social or professional screen behind which the Sun watches. The Moon in Aquarius in the 2nd House would indicate that his livelihood would be in working with others, perhaps with his Sun directing some organisation of a philanthropic nature. He could, for example, be an architect because the Sun is trine to Uranus in the 4th House containing Taurus which is sextile to Pluto in Cancer in the 7th of Partners. This could well mean a deep interest in practical security for his or other families. In short, this is a man deeply concerned with communities where people are cared for. This notion is further enhanced by the point of unease in the 4th and the Sun in opposition to Pluto in the 7th which would suggest a difficult domestic situation both in his parents' and his own home. The effect of this configuration upon a Capricorn in the 12th would be either to seek to escape or to try and conquer the problem. Either way, his Moon would involve him with people, although he would rarely show his inner self. Saturn in Gemini in the 6th would mean careful planning, another indication of a long-training profession, and Pluto and Mars in the 7th suggest a marriage or professional partnership that was full of drama and endless struggle for ascendancy with his wife or professional colleagues. The Pluto indicates that it would be a growth process despite the power confrontations of Mars in Leo which he would deal with by diplomacy rather than war.

Neptune in Virgo in the 8th reveals quite an unexpected element in his psychology. Here a psychic ability and interest in the invisible world is indicated. He would have a small library of occult books alongside the volumes of philosophy, social studies, history and professional reference works. The point of ease in the 10th House would mean that he would eventually be a successful man in the world, making a considerable contribution to society after the many years of struggle (the classic Capricorn pattern). This would be in contrast to his difficult private life. Jupiter in the House of Fellowship would bring powerful allies and friends which, being unaspected by any major angles, would form a social background but never a direct influence on his professional or domestic scene. Jupiter being in Sagittarius, his friends would be people of the same ideals and, with the weak sextile to Mercury, he would enjoy much good conversation, although again he would never reveal his true self or views. The Venus in the 12th might well manifest as either erotic fantasy about ideal love, being in Sagittarius, or more likely a mistress who got on well with his wife through the trine to Mars in the 7th. Indeed, they might be old friends. It could be a discreet but accepted arrangement. So here is FP, a man with a busy professional life and a tough domestic situation who enjoys good company and has a mistress who shares his intense need for privacy, despite an apparently excellent social manner. He also has, because of the Sun and planets in the 12th, 8th and 6th, an interest in matters spiritual. The above description is based upon the latitude thirty degrees North and so FP could live in New Orleans, Cairo or Lhasa, Tibet. This means that the form of the horoscope would be modified to the cultures of those places. Thus the American FP might be part of a philanthropic foundation like the United Nations or working in a well-organised hippy commune while the Egyptian FP might be found organising peasants into collective farms or town planning along the Suez Canal. The Tibetan likewise would be discovered, before the Chinese came, as a lay steward in a monastery or, after the fall of Tibet, as a re-organiser of village life according to the communist view. The Capricornian gift for administration and love of at least some respectable form would assert itself in all three lives and, in this chart, also manifest the social successes and domestic difficulties. In the three cultures, moreover, we would see how a particular psyche, defined by the horoscope, would take on the American, Arab and Tibetan bodies and absorb the surrounding cultures and values. One might, for example, find that the American's Capricorn love of tradition would be expressed in his pride in the ideals of the United States Constitution and his own descent from an original New England family while the Arab would ponder the Koran and try to carry out all the precepts of Islam so that, despite a modern socialist outlook, he would retain many old customs and pass them on to his family. The Tibetan would likewise seek to preserve what he could of old Tibet, perhaps secretly practising Buddhist prayers and keeping in hidden places holy objects or books to remind, when the time came, later generations of what made Tibet one of the most sacred lands in the world. Having created a character, let us now see how a solar progression works.

The first event in FP's life, after his birth with the Sun in ten degrees of Capricorn in the House of Privacy, would be when the progressed Sun crossed the Ascendant at the age of four. This could mean that he began to extend himself outside the home situation. For example, he might have, up till then, simply watched other children at play and not joined in, like standing at the window out of sight while his brothers romped outside. He would have been more shy and reserved than most of his contemporaries. This would change as the Sun entered the 1st House but it would only be a matter of degree. However, the Sun's presence in the House of Appearance would make him conspicuous if only for his great reserve. At five the progressed Sun would be sextile to the place of ease in the House of Achievement and so he would do something that year that would indicate future gifts and capabilities. It might be a remarkable drawing at school of a village with people or a little house built in the back yard which he may have even got others to help him build. This event may have brought him some recognition and admiration for one so young. It would also probably be one of his earliest memories and maybe the thing that unconsciously set his considerable ambition in the general direction of architecture and organisation. In contrast, the same Sun position in trine to his point of unease in the home could have the effect of temporarily alleviating a difficult time within his family circle where his relationship with his parents and brothers was not always harmonious or tranquil. His eighth year would bring the progressed Sun into trine with Uranus but in opposition to Pluto. This suggests a family crisis which would profoundly affect his attitude to marriage in later life. An erratic father is indicated by the Uranus in the 4th; and a strange but enigmatic mother, indicated by Pluto in Cancer in the 7th, might make him seek a similar mother-type figure for a wife because she would offer a security element deeply craved for by the Capricorn who has, as his root, the Cancerian opposite. The events of these years would profoundly affect his later life.

Between eight and fifteen there is no major aspect to the progressing Sun and so one would expect little to happen outside the general laws of childhood and early youth, the epochs of Mercury and Venus. By this time the ego-foundation would have been fairly set and no matter whether it be in the USA, Egypt or Tibet, the same human situation would occur despite the outer garb of culture; and so, by the time the next aspect was engaged, the boy FP would have been leading a relatively uneventful life, providing—and here is where the limits of progressing are revealed—that no major actual planetary events in the general or mundane situation overrode the theoretical scenario suggested by the progression of the personal chart.

At fifteen the progressed Sun would trine Neptune in Virgo in the 8th house of death or hidden matters. The effect could be the death of someone near which opened out the question as to what is the meaning of life, or FP may come across a book; here is the Virgo factor, that considerably changes his outlook. It could be a volume on Christian or Jewish mysticism for the American, the discovery of Ibn Arabi and the Sufis for the Egyptian or the finding of an esoteric text like the

Book of the Dead by the Tibetan. For each of the ways it could be a second deep moment and memory that affected the inner life of the man.

At twenty, when the Sun is progressed into Aquarius, a new phase begins. Here life becomes more sociable and easy and when the Sun begins to approach and apply to conjoin Mercury in his twenty-sixth year there is no holding back. He travels a lot, learns a great deal about people and, from his inherent sense of history, collects a vast amount of background information about societies great and small. Nothing but hard work happens for six years but, from his thirty-second year on, when the Sun sextiles Jupiter in the House of Fellowship, he meets and acquires many friends with similar views. They are attached to him in deep affection and good will and balance the unseen solitariness and hard graft of work

At thirty-five, when the Sun is squared to the ascending and descending nodes, he has a professional set-back and a bad time at home—perhaps his father or mother is ill and he has to take on family responsibilities. It is a difficult period. Three years later, when the Sun is squared to Uranus, a second blow occurs with perhaps the death of a parent and a radical change in his domestic arrangements.

At forty things take a distinct turn as the Sun now sextiles Venus indicating a love affair, in which a woman is actually allowed into his private life, and then marriage as Saturn is trined. Such a late marriage is not unusual for a Capricorn. The Saturn in the 6th indicates that his wife was or is in the same profession; as it is in Gemini she might well have been his assistant for some years. However, all is not well because, in the year of marriage, Mars in Leo in the 7th House is in opposition to the progressed Sun, so that conflict is generated out of his own and his wife's desire for status and his inner need to retire periodically from public appearance for recreation and contemplation. At the age of forty-four the progressed Sun enters the 2nd House and he, at last, after many years' struggle, begins to acquire wealth both material and intellectual—Aquarius being an Air sign. This situation is enhanced two years later when the Sun conjoins the natal Moon and brings a considerable reputation for him in his field of work. He is perhaps acknowledged as the expert both in practice and theory on social and housing problems.

At fifty, the progressed Sun enters Pisces and the next phase of life begins. Gradually his relationship to his work, ideas and possessions changes from just intellectual to include the emotional. He has moral doubts about well-tried concepts and at fifty-two, when the Sun trines his Midheaven, he sees his achievements in a religious context. This growing aspect of his nature turns his spiritual inquiry of many years to consider what his work and profession is really about. Again, because there are no major aspects, nothing happens for at least eight years but, as the progressed Sun trines his natal Sun, he receives with slowly increasing force a revelation about the truth of his own nature. This creates a very deep change, although only a few know of its advent because it is hidden in the 12th House. At sixty-two, when the Sun is squared to Jupiter in the House of Fellowship, he undergoes a painful rearrangement of relationships with his life-long companions, seeing them perhaps as nothing but idealising talkers and not realising doers, because there are no strong aspects to apply the energy practically. At sixty-five, when the Sun is sextile to his point of unease and trine to his point of ease, a shift of situation makes both his domestic and his professional scenes harmonise for a brief period. At sixty-eight, the Sun is sextile to Uranus and trine to Pluto, so that the home or marriage scene is positively transformed by some extraordinary event, such as the death of his wife. At three score years and ten we will leave FP with the progressed Sun squared to Saturn and Venus which could mean a final period of cynical reflection before death, if there were no spiritual growth, or a renewed, pleasant and contemplative stage of work continuing into a rich Capricornian old age, if deep inner transformation had taken place.

Now, all the foregoing is entirely speculative and fictional but what it does demonstrate is how a set of psychological principles are activated to create events as the Sun aspects them. Again, it must be repeated that this, like all real progressions, is only speculative anyway because it is based upon an artificial device. Referring to progressions of actual people brings out a most important point, that in a genuine chart all the celestial bodies are placed in a set of preordained rhythms which are expressing, at a given moment, the current state of Creation and Evolution in relation to the Beginning and End of Time. This means, unlike a fictional chart, that every real horoscope fits into an already existing scheme that is slowly unfolding throughout the Universe at large, in the Milky Way in particular and within our Solar system in detail; so that nearly all the events on Earth are providentially interwoven and set out to manifest in certain times in Existence. Thus as a spirit is incarnated it is slotted into a particular place and time to enact a cosmic destiny. As Ecclesiastes puts it, 'To everything there is

Prediction: A Sample Life

a season and a time to every purpose under the Heaven: a time to be born, and a time to die; a time to plant, and a time to pluck up that which is planted; a time to kill, and a time to heal; a time to break down, and a time to build up; a time to weep, and a time to laugh; a time to mourn, and a time to dance; a time to cast away stones, and a time to gather stones together; a time to embrace, and a time to refrain from embracing; a time to get, and a time to lose; a time to keep, and a time to cast away; a time to rend, and a time to sew; a time to keep silence, and a time to speak; a time to love, and a time to hate; a time of war, and a time of peace.'

The purpose of each phase is development of the being and this, as we have observed from life, is not always through easy lessons or quick solutions. Goodness, knowledge and courage have to be tested and proved or they are only potential. To become actual they are made to pass through the vicissitudes of life and fate so that the being expressing them may actually experience good in the face of evil, knowledge in contrast to ignorance and courage in the midst of danger. Thus each life has its talents and tests. These tendencies, however, are not only factors in the chart that indicates the fate to be lived. Also present are the results of previous incarnations and the tendencies, both good and bad, acquired during the current life. One of the most common manifestations of the evil is the phenomenon of disease. This is the subject of the next chapter.

Figure 27—AFFLICTION
According to tradition, different parts of the body are ruled by various signs and sefirot. Thus the Moon and Yesod relate to the ego, persona and sexuality. If the natal Moon is afflicted in the chart, or just at the moment, it will affect these psychological and physical functions. If such a situation persists, then illness will manifest to a greater or lesser degree. This applies to all the bodily functions which resonate with their psychological counterparts. (Medieval woodcut).

13. Disease

Disease, as the word suggests, means dis-ease, that is unease. This title, in our frame of reference, indicates any malady ranging from a mild intellectual disability, like being unable to remember one's twelve times table, to terminal cancer. The origin of such disorders may be broadly said to be internal or external, or psychological or physical. Further, the generation of disease may be inherent or acquired, brought about by the person's psychological or physical over-activity or non-activity, or have a malady imposed from without by accident or infection. As should now be appreciated, seeing that everything in the Universe is interrelated, there is no such thing as an 'accident' in the accepted sense of the word. There is the meeting of apparently unrelated lines of development and there is the sudden appearance of an unexpected event but with a deeper knowledge, or at least a sense of fate, these happenings are perceived as inevitable or prefigured events in a life. Let us examine the various levels of such phenomena so as to see the astrological mechanism of acute and chronic physical and psychological diseases and the significance of accidents.

Beginning with the coarsest world, we physically inherit the bodily strengths and weaknesses of our race. Thus if we are Eskimos our resistance to TB is less than a white person's, while a European is more prone to some tropical diseases and would easily succumb to an illness that would only mildly affect an African. Next we have the inherent physical tendencies of our nation or people. For example, the Jews have a very high propensity for nervous disorders while the Norwegians suffer from a particular kind of cancer. This same phenomenon of cancer, but in a different bodily area, occurs amongst the Parsees of India while certain African tribes are afflicted by maladies unknown elsewhere in the world. The causes of such illnesses are partly to do with location, climate and diet and partly to do with centuries, if not millennia, of psychological attitudes. For example, the Parsees' problem is generated by the lack of marriage outside the clan, because of the demand for strict purity of family, while the

Jewish inclination to nervous diseases is the understandable result of centuries of insecurity and persecution. All of us inherit the inbred constitution of our people and those who are half and half from mixed marriages have the strength and weaknesses of both. This level constitutes the general fatal pattern of our tribal group and its state of development.

Tribal constitutional legacy is given to a child at the moment of conception in that, in the genes and chromosomes of the parents, the medical history of both families is transferred and blended into the fertilised cell. As the child will develop the father's build or the mother's complexion, so it will advance or retard the family tendency to heart trouble or kidney disease and so on. Superimposed upon this is the Ascendant that modifies the racial and family physical characteristics. Thus the Gemini Ascendant will enhance any nervous or chest complaints inherent in the body while Leo rising will increase any strength or weakness of the heart. A Capricornian Ascendant will influence the slightest family tendency to rheumatism or skin disease as Cancer rising will affect a propensity to breast and stomach disorders. The basis of these conclusions, it will be remembered, is the traditional notion that the various parts of the body are associated with the signs of the Zodiac. Likewise the planets are traditionally related to different organs. For example, the reason why Leo is associated with the heart is because the Sun is its ruler and the heart is the all-powerful Sun of the body's Solar system of organs. In a similar manner Virgo, whose ruler is the negative or receptive aspect of Mercury, is related to the nervous system and intestines, both of which maintain the optimum level of working proficiency in the biological machine. The significance of these astrological and physical interactions was discovered empirically over many centuries and used by the medical profession until the seventeenth century in Europe to diagnose and treat disease.

Because there is a connection between the subtle and the physical Worlds, it will be seen that a particular balance of the psychological anatomy will have a distinct influence on the body. Thus while the physiology may inherit certain strengths and weaknesses from its biological line, these may be undermined or checked by the nature of the psyche. For example, supposing a man has inherited a strong physical constitution but has the Sun, Moon, Mercury, Venus and Mars in Virgo in the 6th House. This will have the effect of making, if the other planets are in bad aspect, a basically healthy man into a nervous, health-preoccupied fretter who would see only his physical imperfections, treating each ache and pain with meticulous care from his enormous selection of remedies. While this is an extreme example, it illustrates the influence of the psyche over the body. The net effect would be eventual illness, imaginary or otherwise. Here is where we begin to perceive how the subtle body moulds fatal attitudes and subsequent events of that lifetime.

Let us suppose a person has Mars in Libra, where it is in detriment, and that planet and sign are found in the 4th House of security. This would indicate that emotional stress in the home would generate kidney trouble, seeing that Libra rules these organs, and that debilitated and divided emotions would create a weak and placating psychological attitude to parents or spouse. This could, of course, be offset by some support from the other planets, or a deliberate and conscious choice to develop and overcome the weakness, but we will discuss this later. The point here is that a psychological condition such as, in this case, confused and repressed anger will create, in the body, much wear and tear leading to many waste poisons with which the kidneys have to deal. Over a long time the kidney capacity, however good due to inheritance and an excellent diet, will be reduced through sheer overwork. We all know people who eat health foods and yet deny life and its involvements to such a degree that they make themselves ill. This is how disease is often generated.

Another way of looking at the interaction of the psyche on the body is when a person has, say, Saturn squared to the Sun. This situation, seen by the perceptive astrologer, is when certain formalised intellectual concepts act as a deep unconscious constraint on the ability to be open and honest. For example, particular religious, philosophical or political notions, imbibed into the unconscious over many years, about love or truth or freedom may hold back the person's desire to express affection openly, see reality or experience the world outside the rigid bounds of a formal religion or class-oriented politics. The long-term effect will be a constriction by the psychological Sun upon the physical heart of the person, so that he slowly becomes stiffened, then atrophied into a closed state where the strain of a darkened Solar principle will eventually manifest in the chronic cardiac diseases associated with those stress conditions. Again depending upon which sign they are in, the other planets and Moon can mitigate or increase the affliction. Thus a Sun in Aries, where it is exalted, trine to Jupiter in Sagittarius, where it is most powerful, will offset to a degree a Saturn in Leo, the sign governing the heart, where Saturn is in detriment. The placing of

Figure 28—HEALING
Here a physician consults the astrological situation and relates it to the patient's birth chart. There is a close astrological correspondence in both mental and physical health in esoteric medicine, which has been almost lost, although some modern medicine does acknowledge psychosomatic disorders. Many diseases originating in the mind need an astrological diagnosis as well as the conventional medical, as of old. This combined view was lost in the so-called Age of Reason, when the esoteric dimension of health was forgotten. (16th century woodcut).

DISEASE   121

the signs and planets in the Houses will, of course, indicate the areas in life where the tension would be expected. Thus if the Sun, for example, were in the 10th House where it would be squared and oppressed by Saturn in the 7th, then trouble with business partners or wife would be the outward manifestation of the cause of the illness.

To illustrate by actual example the principle of the subtle or planetary bodies' effect upon the physical, let us take a well-known historical figure who passed through a major crisis period and suffered an acute condition directly related to a planetary situation. President Richard Nixon, who we have already seen in relation to the horoscope of the United States, had Sun in Capricorn in the 5th House of fame and power and Moon in Aquarius in the 6th of health and day-to-day work. During the latter months of his term of office he was under considerable pressure on all sides from the inevitable US military defeat in Vietnam, the Watergate exposure of the seamy side of government, a massive economic recession and a general assault on his image as President of a country founded upon the ideal of political integrity.

As will be quickly perceived, the ambitious and tenacious Capricorn Sun would seek to hold on to office as long as possible, no matter how much ego-Moon was pounded. During the period we are examining, however, Saturn, as noted in the section on the United States horoscope, was in mid-Cancer and in opposition to Nixon's Sun. This aspect not only hammered the United States as a nation but beat at Nixon himself as it advanced up to oppose his Sun. His Moon, already squared by Saturn in his horoscope, was also under direct fire over July-August 1974 from the Sun in Leo. Moreover, Mercury in Leo from 6 to 20 August did not help his ego-image either, because his working methods would be, and were, exposed to the world at large, greatly to his political and personal detriment. While this major pressure was building up upon his psyche, his body began to react.

On 24 June, the day after the Sun entered Cancer, he was diagnosed as having phlebitis which is an inflammation of a vein associated with a blood clot. Seen astrologically Aquarius, which his natal Moon occupied, is associated with not only the legs but the Leo-Aquarius combination of heart and circulation. Phlebitis of the left leg was confirmed in July when the Sun, having passed through opposition to his Sun, then moved on to oppose his Moon. In August he was brought down by public and government pressure to resign on Thursday 8 August when the Sun was coming to maximum opposition to his natal Moon and the Moon in Aries was squaring his natal Sun. A few weeks later, as the Sun was about to enter Libra and begin to square his Sun, and Saturn was exactly opposite his Sun, he was hospitalised for treatment. He left hospital in early October but was re-hospitalised on the 23rd as the Sun was about to enter Scorpio, the surgeon's sign, which was square to his Moon. On the 29th of the month, when the Moon was again in Aries and squared to his Sun, he suffered from a severe post-operative vascular shock that placed his life in the balance. He survived and left hospital on 14 November when both Sun and Moon were in Scorpio and Saturn began to move off opposition to his Sun.

From the foregoing it will be seen how periods of great stress in the macrocosm can impose pressure, first upon the subtle body through its sympathetic resonance (for want of a better expression) and then on to the carnal vehicle which will manifest the disharmony physically in the related zodiacal body zones. The remedy, ideally, is in preventative action at the psychological level, so that the strain is not transmitted down into the body. This, however, requires a great deal of self-knowledge and personal discipline which few individuals have. For most people the cure lies in the treatment of the symptoms and not the causes, for which modern medicine supplies a relatively primitive set of surgical and chemical solutions. Ancient medicine, with its acceptance of the subtle body, took into account the planetary factors and diagnosed disease according to both physical and celestial evidence because there was a clear correspondence between certain maladies and afflicting planetary principles. While ancient methods of treatment may seem unscientific to the modern surgeon and physician, they were based upon a very precise set of subtle laws. For example, Culpeper's seventeenth-century herbal remedies were based upon certain plants and their relationship to particular signs and planets. Thus, for instance, the caraway plant associated with Virgo assisted digestion while the dock, astrologically connected with Pisces, strengthens the liver which is governed by Jupiter, the ruler of Pisces. Lavender, a herb of Gemini, was applied to headaches and heartsease, an Aquarian plant, clearly related to opposing an afflicted Sun. All these remedies were used in relation to the natal horoscope of the patient and the current situation in the sky which was highly relevant as the Nixon example illustrates so well.

Psychological troubles are different from physical disease because they are seated in a different World. These are strict disorders of the subtle being, although there are physical side effects and symptoms to be found in the body as a result—like the chemical imbalance of the brain or the inability to move. Here we must distinguish between cause and effect. Astrologically, mental disorders can be classified by sign or planets. For example, an afflicted Saturn will generate a tendency to severe depression whereas an over-active Mars will create an aggressive manic condition. A very badly placed Mercury will encourage neurotic confusion while an apparently extremely well-aspected Venus could make for excessive promiscuity, nymphomania and its subsequent venereal diseases (hence the name). Moon in Leo, but unsuitably placed and badly aspected, is conducive to megalomania and Uranus, particularly afflicted, can breed the type of madness associated with creative genius. Both of the double signs of Gemini and Pisces are particularly subject to schizophrenia. So too is Libra. This condition is often precipitated by an unconnected Moon which has no aspects with any of the other celestial bodies. Indeed, any unaspected planet or luminary can have the problem of isolation and its attendant gift of objectivity or curse of negative involvement. The classic case is the person with an unaspected Moon-Cancer in the 12th House who retreats into his private world of egocentric creations and lives out a fantasy wherein he is the central pivot about which everything orbits. That is why the ancients called this form of malady 'lunacy.'

Finally, let us now examine injury apparently precipitated from outside the physical and psychological organism. First, there is no such thing as an accident. All events are exactly as they are because, since the beginning of Time, the Universe has been unfolding under law. Thus in analogue, if we throw a stone into a pond, its flight path will conform to the interaction of the laws of gravity, air pressure and humidity and wind upon the weight, mass and shape of the stone. This means it can hit only one predetermined spot. When it breaks the surface of the water, the stone will then come under another set of laws that will govern its sinking to a precise place at the bottom of the pond. The effects of such an event upon the pond's life, even down to its smallest bacteria and finest mud, will be just as precise as everything settles itself back, but not quite, to equilibrium. So it is with providential or so-called accidental intrusions into our lives.

The movement of the Universe impels everything continually to change and so happenings occur—but under very definite laws and with great precision. This is because at the lower end of Existence there are many more laws to monitor the level of underdeveloped beings, in case they err too far and are destroyed. This does not mean to say that there is no free will. This privilege, however, belongs to the area of inner consciousness and not to external events. Everything that happens in the outside world is more or less fixed as the falling stone's path. Even the so-called moments of history, when big decisions are made, are the effects and result of cosmic laws. No government or individual commands, they simply respond to the ebb and flow of celestial tides that prompt mundane events which contain the rise and fall of peoples, the growth or decay of societies and the forming and dissolving of families enmeshed deep in the midst of a national, global and cosmic drama. Thus, if an accident occurs it is not at random but the result of the great event generating a smaller event to coincide with another small happening at a particular point in time. Thus two global economic systems oppose, nations confront, armies fight, two soldiers meet and one dies. In the case of the individual development or degeneration it is a different matter. Here is the action of free will or the work of some higher principle.

A man is injured in a car crash. Perhaps his Uranus in Virgo is squared by Mercury. Another man in the same vehicle is unharmed. (His Gemini Sun perhaps is conjunct with Mercury.) Why? Because it is, for most, a situation in which both would be hurt. The reason why it is different for different people is because such factors of fate as reward, punishment, opportunity and testing come into action and this is the operation of the upper Worlds. I say that for most it would be a fatal situation but there are individuals who can pass untouched through the most dreadful events. These are people operating under the laws of the spirit and destiny. Such examples are found in the saints who walk through plague or war-ridden areas and are protected. People such as this are obviously very rare but they do exist.

Most of us are under fatal or planetary law. So it is that when we contract, by external contact, this infection or are injured in that situation, it is not an accident but the result of our path through life that brings us to be in a certain place at a certain time with a particular susceptibility to that disease or proneness to accident. The proof is that there are often others also present who were more deeply infected or hurt as badly. This indicates the cardinal fact that most of life is an inevitable unfolding and therefore prefigured if nothing is done to overcome the blinkered fixity that governs our lives. As one spiritual teacher said, 'You do not realise how all your physical habits and rigid attitudes of mind lock you mechanically into a fatal pattern. How can it be otherwise if a person does not recognise just how asleep he is psychologically and spiritually?' Again and again this raises the issue of free will and the ability to change fate and thus avoid disease or accident and perhaps even death. However, before this skill can be gained much self-knowledge is necessary. In kabbalistic astrology this begins when one first studies one's own chart and relates self-knowledge to external and internal events. This exercise is the art of 'election' which is the first stage of choice. However, because the Universe is founded upon Divine Justice and Mercy, there are moments in which the most dimly conscious of people can practise the right of choice. These moments usually occur in fatal crises so that no person is ever denied the privilege of free will.

Figure 29—CONFRONTATION
Every fate has a moment of crisis when there is a critical set of aspects in the birth chart and the person's circumstances. Here, a man confronts his dragon, an archetype of his particular demon. He has to fight this shadow side of his nature or control the primitive neurotic drives within. In this case, Mars—or Judgement—has to combat this destructive element that could ruin his life. From a kabbalistic viewpoint this is a test and initiation. (Alchemical image, 17th century).

14. Moments of Crisis and Decision

Some celestial rhythms are great and some are small. Some have a daily effect and others a monthly, seasonal or yearly unit of time. Some rhythms stretch over decades and some over hundreds and thousands of years in cycle. All, however, are woven into the fabric of Time as a single recognisable fusion known as *Now*. *Now* is the Eternal present, the ever-moving instant that was begun at the beginning of Time when the cosmic processes of Creation and Evolution were set in motion. *Now* is the only reality. Both the past and unmanifest future are contained in the *Now*. For us who live in the physical World, *Now* is the physical manifestation of what happens in the upper Worlds. It is the reality for us because, while we may examine the past and speculate about the future, it is the *Now* of this moment on Earth to which we can directly relate, learn from and experience. However, with insight into the past we may, by looking at the balance of forces in the upper Worlds in the present moment, speculate and act correctly and with advantage in the future. This is the basis of two branches of astrology known as Horary and Judicial astrology.

Horary astrology is the art of posing questions and then examining the horoscope of the moment when the question arose. The nature of the question is usually a matter of deep concern to the querent to whom the question must have a significant meaning. On the ordinary level, such a question might arise about a missing person or a distant event connected with the questioner. The method was used in the old days to find out the fate of overdue travellers because, by examining the chart of the moment, certain omens, like Moon in Scorpio in the 8th House squared to one of the malefics, could indicate death. The method is not unlike the *I Ching* or *Book of Changes* that operates upon the law of synchronicity, that is, that everything is related to everything else so that a happening here is responded to there, and so it is possible, by using a set of first principles, to focus upon events in the subtle World that will inform one about distant events in the physical. Horary astrology operates the same way, except that it uses an astrological set of criteria to indicate the situation. The issue here, however, is not so much that it works in the hands of a skilled and objective astrologer because, unlike the crystallised verse and commentary of the *I Ching*, an astrologer's judgement can be biased, but that the moment of question expresses the state of the celestial tides and the particular configuration of cycles and influences of that moment out of which one may assess events.

The implication of the above is enormous. It means that it is possible, in theory at least, to know what is happening on the big scale and therefore what might follow and plan things accordingly. This is the function of Judicial astrology. Now, astrologers over the ages have been employed by kings, generals and merchants for just this reason. Indeed, that is why their profession was encouraged. There was a time, for instance, when no king would allow himself to be crowned except at the moment recommended by his astrologers because such a point of beginning would have a distinct effect upon his reign. Nor would any general begin a battle without consulting his staff astrologer who would calculate the moment when the celestial forces would run in his master's favour. This would be done by relating the general's horoscope to the current situation and selecting the moment when the Moon and Mars were in the right combination to aid the judgement and determination of the general and his army. Likewise, a shrewd merchant would wait not only upon the sea tides to send his ship forth but also upon the position of the Moon and Jupiter being well aspected, if possible, in the 2nd and 10th Houses of possessions and achievement. On the more personal level, the same procedure is applied to the individual life at crucial moments but this is more subtle and complex than the mundane affairs of politics, war and commerce which are subject to general, rather than particular, law. The concerns of an individual are of quite a different order because an assessment by Judicial astrology is useful not only concerning events in the physical World but to examine psychological and spiritual crises and turning points in life.

Everyone has periods of crisis in their lives. The first is Earthly birth or Ascendant crisis when there is the enormous effort and shock of being transferred fully into the physical World. At this point there is the possibility of not making the arrival and, without a little skilled encouragement from those present at the birth, there would be, as there used to be, many discarnate souls who would back away into the subtle World again. The Lunar crisis occurs at the transition point between babyhood and childhood when the person first detaches

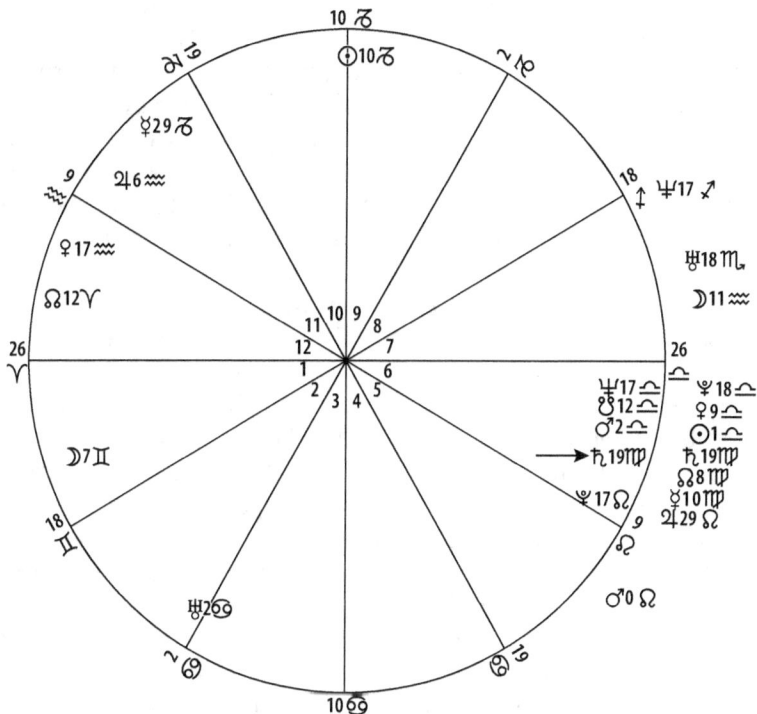

Figure 30—SATURN RETURN
When any planet returns to its original position, a new cycle begins. This is clearly seen when Saturn, in its roughly twenty-nine year orbit, conjoins its original place in the birth chart. The result is often either the breakdown of a set of ideas or their reinforcment. From the viewpoint of development this is crucial. A person at, say, around thirty can crystallise or move to a new epoch. In this case, health and work will be critically affected. He would stay in a humdrum job and slowly atrophy or develop into a fulfilling profession and a healthy regime. (Halevi).

himself from his mother and begins to relate to other children and thus begin the Mercurial confrontations. Later there is the Venus crisis of adolescence when the person has to cope with love and its attendant agonies and ecstasies. Later still, there is the Solar stage when one is required to be fully responsible for oneself and so on, as we progress through the seven planetary phases of life. Now these events are of a fixed order. They may come sooner or later in individuals but come they must, or the experience of life is incomplete. Here it is important to recognise that they are as inevitable as our example of the stone falling into the pond and sinking to a particular place at the bottom. The earlier or later manifestation of the crisis is due to the peculiarities of a particular chart. For example the Aries subject will, because of his or her nature, be into the game of love long before the Capricorn who will also take longer to find his Solar identity.

While the inevitability of fatal events is a fact, they should not be viewed as an absolutely rigid sequence. This is only true of those who choose to live a totally mechanical life. Thus, although the general form of a life is determined, one can see that points of crisis also create possibility of change because such moments, pleasant and unpleasant, usually awaken most people out of a deep psychological slumber of habitual patterns into the reality of their lives and its possibilities.

Let us examine the astrological principles involved by looking at an easily recognised crisis experienced by those about to enter their thirtieth year. This is called the 'Saturn return' by astrologers. By this is meant that the planet of understanding and reflection has gone its full orbit and now conjoins its original natal position. This happens at about the age of twenty-nine. While it may be noted that all the other planets inside Saturn's orbit have already done this, the crises precipitated by Mars and Jupiter are of much shorter duration and period. Mars, for example, returns roughly every two years and so emotional decisions have already been occurring throughout childhood and youth, while Jupiter's twelve-year cycle provides two major periods of emotional expansion at the beginning of adolescence and at twenty-four.

The significance of Saturn is that it reveals, often under duress, all the results of personal performance in the growing phase of life. Childhood has gone and youth is about to fade. This realisation usually makes a person take stock of their talents and their actual capacity. They may see, in Saturnine reflection, how they have made their dream begin to come true or their fantasies dissolve in failure and they

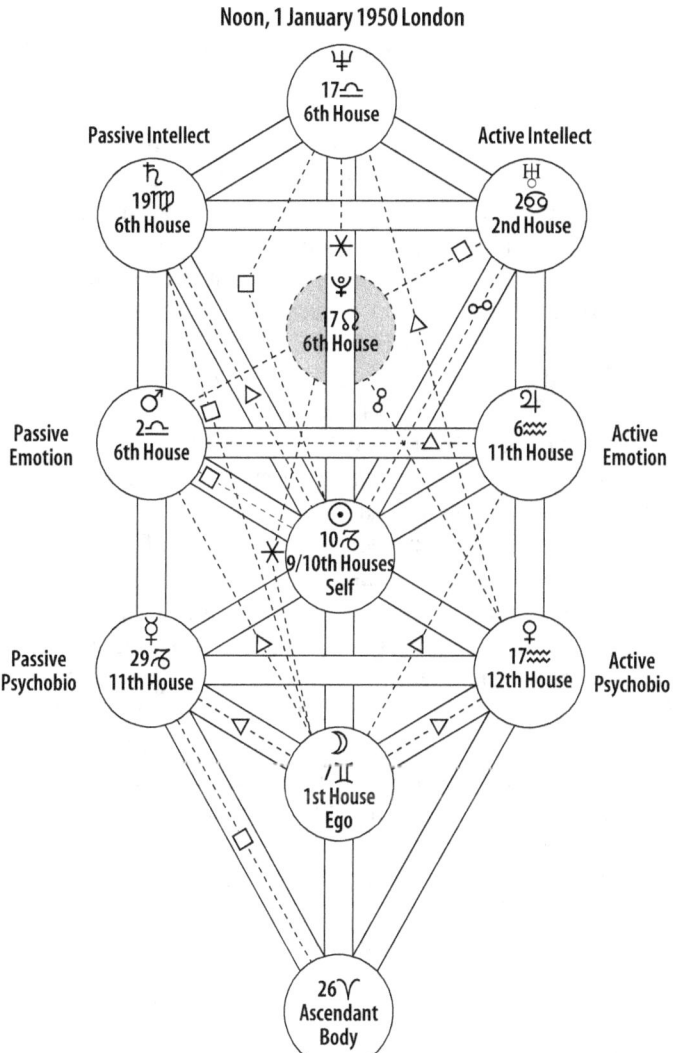

Figure 31—PSYCHOLOGY
In this Tree the horoscope indicates, for example, a variable ego. The Geminian Moon, being in the 1st House and having so many aspects to different parts of the mind, would generate a kaleidoscopic personality. Flashes of insight from Uranus would be supported by impulsive descisions from Mars. But these would be opposed by a nit-picking Saturnine philosophy. The Self, embodied by a Capricornian Sun in the 10th House, would steady this trend but frustrate great ambition by erratic behaviour. This would be a major factor in the fate and the lesson to be learned. (Halevi).

will, if they can, utilise Saturn's long view, anticipate how far they might go in their job and how they can prepare the next step. For a woman it might be the period when she takes her first deep look at the state of her marriage. She will now see, with an experienced eye, that the running of a home and bringing up of children was nothing like the mythology of married bliss. She will observe that most of her life, be it professional or domestic, is in fact hard work and responsibility with little time for the pleasures expected of an extended love affair. For a married man it might be a Saturnine appreciation of the great labour involved in bringing up a family and forging a career as he perceives the long middle period haul ahead before he achieves his ambition. For the unmarried it can be a gloomy time of recognising the possibility of no marriage or the acceptance of a partnership that is not based upon a romantic ideal. Or it can be that time when the dreams of youth begin either to fade or start to be turned into reality as Saturn teaches its practical philosophy.

For those who do not see below the surface of events and their implication, such a crisis can make their worst faults manifest as the weaknesses in a horoscope come into play and harden the negative side of Saturn's influence. Many lives have been set, by this Saturn period, to become almost entirely ones of drudgery in home and job. For those who do not just live off the dreams, memories and desires of a now-past age of childhood and youth the situation is full of new possibilities. These can only occur if one can recognise what is actually happening. Here is where the full worth of Judicial astrology is applied. Let us take, for example, the Saturn return of an imaginary person born, for the sake of argument, at noon on 1 January 1950 in London (see chart, Figure 30).

Here we have someone with immense ambition, due to the position of the Sun at the Midheaven in Capricorn, and great personal charm due to Gemini in the 1st House. Aries Ascendant would give him a powerful drive and, in conjunction with the rest of the horoscope, one might expect him to be a distinguished journalist, a correspondent in diplomatic and political matters, knowing all the right people round the world. His ability to make contacts and exploit situations both personal and international would bring him considerable fame and his well-informed accounts of political events would be full of a sense of history and scale. Jupiter in Aquarius in the 11th House would grant him very powerful friends sympathetic to the political left even though he, as a Capricorn, would be inclined to the right of the political spectrum. However, his Mercurial Moon would enable him to be flexible in viewpoint and skilful in questioning. Probing with the audacity of his Ascendant, he would get where few other correspondents would dare to intrude.

With Saturn, Mars, Neptune and Pluto in the 6th House his health would not be perfect but he would drive himself on, sometimes ignoring warning symptoms of disease. Mercury in Capricorn in the 11th would mean many acquaintances in government and Venus in the 12th, in Aquarius, indicates a variety of interesting but discreet love affairs. Uranus in Cancer on the cusp of the 3rd House would lead to an irregular form of income, such as a freelance journalist might expect, and a genius for digging up remarkable facts about closed societies and cabinet secrets. His ascending and descending Nodes show an ease in his moments of privacy, when he can relax, and an area of difficulty in his actual working conditions and health which one might expect of a travelling man. Here then, in brief, is the man's character. Now let us move on into the future and see how the Saturn return is likely to affect his period of reappraisal.

Taking only some of the aspects because it is, in fact, a highly detailed operation, we will see the broad outline of the period in his thirtieth year. Firstly the return of Saturn to its original position, which begins on September 25 1979, will bring up the issue of health. He will suffer from some kind of constriction of the intestines; the position being in Virgo and broadly square to the Moon in Gemini. This means the nervous wear and tear has begun to take its toll. However, being trine to the natal Sun, his ambition will thrust him on—unless he sees what lies before him in illness as he overloads his physical organism. This return position will also mean that he is irritated, and irritates his professional colleagues, either by his or their critical comments based upon his remarkable success, and possible arrogance, or their jealousy. This again will be an indication that he must take a deep look at himself at work.

Mars, at this time, will be coming into opposition to his natal Jupiter and therefore he may, because it is in Leo, be a little over-confident of his relationships with the powerful. This could lead to trouble. Moreover, the 1979 Uranus position will be squared to his Venus and so there are likely to be some sudden disruptions in his intimate life. Further, Pluto conjunct his natal Neptune in Libra is also bound to affect his relationships, both professional and private, transforming them either into an estrangement or something deeper.

Here again is an area of crucial choice. The Sun conjunct Mars in Libra on the day that Saturn comes exactly into return emphasises the relationship area and his difficulty in making a decision about how he relates. For example, he may have found it difficult to commit himself to a marriage and be unsure whether to pull out of a professional partnership when his integrity says he should. 'They might be useful,' his Geminian Moon-ego would say; and his afflicted Mars would not help his judgement. By now we begin to see a man at a very crucial point in his career. The seeds of his strengths and weaknesses, both physical and psychological, are beginning to bear their first fruits.

Most men caught up in this situation ignore the signs that can bring them down. If, in this case, the man recognises what is a physical threat and takes more rest to offset the possibility of ill health, he may yet still realise nothing about the psychological principles that are generating the condition. These could, if not understood, eventually destroy his private relationships and the achievements of his professional life. This is obviously a very important piece of self-knowledge and, if one of his colleagues or women does not providentially face him with it, he may never know what hit him when the next major crisis of Uranus in opposition to its original position comes into focus in March 1988. Such an event might well make or break him, both in health and profession.

The significance of the above story for kabbalistic astrologers is that, by examining the period when Saturn returns to its natal position, one can ascertain the problems to be resolved as well as seeing the fulfilment of expectations. The possibility of such knowledge is given spontaneously in crisis by Providence, if not by deliberate consultation of the natal chart, so that the continuous way to perfection can be practised. The conscious action of self-evolution can, alas, only be implemented by those who wish to take on the full responsibility for their lives. Most people drift along, totally unaware that they are at the mercy of cosmic forces which move them to and fro in the ebb and flow of subtle tides. For evidence of this phenomenon of mass will-less-ness, witness the events of the two World Wars. Millions were drawn from their factories, farms and offices into a vortex of the national violence without a struggle and many went to fight and die under a pressure which they could have resisted but did not. This is the meaning of being under general law. Only individuals with enough self- or Solar consciousness and developed free will can recognise and use these cosmic tides, instead of being swept along by them. Such individuals are not born but are created by themselves over a long period of self-discipline which begins with recognising that their lives have an inherent significance beyond filling the Ascendant's biological needs or the Moon's social roles. This brings us to the development of choice, leading to free will and decision.

15. Degrees of Choice

We have touched upon the theme of choice from time to time but now let us begin to examine what it really means in detail, to observe that there are, in fact, degrees of choice. First, it has been established that as the Universe unfolds it follows a hierarchical series of interpenetrating influences that manifest in a chain throughout all four Worlds, down through the Milky Way and the Solar system to life on Earth. Nature, which is composed of three orders of cellular beings is, in varying degrees, from plants up through animals to man, sensitive to cosmic influences. Generally speaking, the two lower levels respond slowly to celestial changes but mankind, being the most evolved and particularly responsive to the subtle World, reacts sometimes dramatically to occurrences within the planetary World. These reactions can take the form of mass movements, that is, manifest in events like war, social revolution and great migrations. Most of humanity, like plants and animals, is totally unaware of these celestial pressures but there are, as said, some people who are conscious of cosmic weather and adopt and utilise it for individual and general progress. They have that very rare possession—full free will. However, before we can begin to comprehend this level of humanity we must study the physical, vegetable and animal parts of man to see how there are degrees of free will which are influenced by bodily desire, psychological consciousness and spiritual choice.

The physical body a person inhabits is composed of a myriad of cells that have been developed by Nature into a set of interacting systems operating a multiplicity of actions, ranging from digesting food to making a delicate piece of jewellery. This organic machine, moreover, can for example, correct its own temperature, make allowances for humidity and even repair major disorders within its own mechanism. All this it does without the consent of the tenant. Further, it has, under certain conditions, a decided set of views like the desire to avoid pain, pursue pleasure and run away from any threat of destruction. The obvious conclusion and a little self observation confirms this—that the body has a distinct and powerful will of its own. The classic

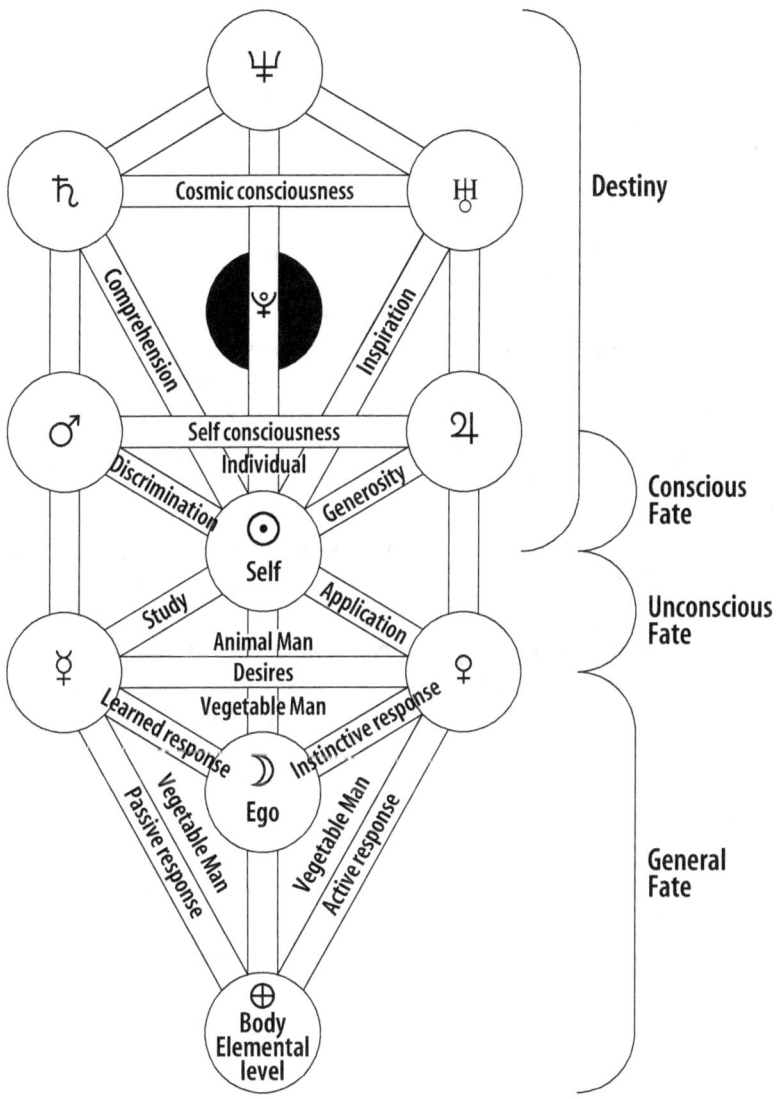

Figure 32 — CHOICE
Depending upon the level of a person's psychological evolution, their fate would come under the general law of mass movement, struggle to be successful or be a true individual. The vegetable level constitutes about ninety percent of people with the animal making up around nine percent. The remaining one percent are those who are conscious of their fate and know what their destiny is. They are the spearhead of human evolution. In a population of 50 million, this would be half a million. (Halevi).

example is the biological need to eat. When a person is very hungry they will, unless they are a remarkable individual, be forced by this will to work and in desperate circumstances steal and even kill for survival. Thus we observe that the body has a considerable influence, consciously or unconsciously, in what motivates most people. This is the real power of the Ascendant.

Seen in astrological detail, the Ascendant in relation to physical desires and aversions gives the body a particular elemental quality. The Earth sign Ascendants, for example, have a cold dryness, the Watery a slightly clammy quality while the Air signs possess a wet heat and the Fire a radiance and dryness. These elemental qualities of a body not only give a distinct feeling of weight, fluidity and vitality but make the person seek a certain physical condition conducive to the health or avoid those which are antipathetic to the organism. Thus a Leo Ascendant is often a compulsive Sun seeker while the Saturnine Capricorn is inclined to dry shady places. These bodily needs indicate certain limits of natural preference which actually eliminate the principle of choice. Under a similar set of elemental laws, people of the same body type are attracted to or disinterested in those that relate or do not relate to their physical element. Generally speaking Earth and Fire body-types have little attraction for each other, in that one becomes smothered and the other burnt, while Water and Air produce a drowning froth. Unless there is an override of planets and luminaries in sympathetic signs, the physical encounter will be a non-event. Thus there is little choice here or, indeed, much evidence of free will in whom we attract and repel just on a physical basis.

Besides the desire to survive there is the vegetable impulse of the organism to mate and propagate. This is one of the most powerful wills there is. Indeed, after seeking a secure place to live and enough to eat, the theme of mating is the greatest preoccupation of most of humanity. It is not only expressed in the tribal meetings at the local clearing, city dance-hall, social or high society gatherings where the endless intrigues of love are played out but in the arts, fashion, business and everything to do with the theme of man and woman. While this is an obvious fact of life, it illustrates the power of sex and how it persuades people to place themselves into a state of submission wherein they will not only enjoy love's pleasures but endure its pains and take on the heavy responsibility of creating homes, bearing and bringing up children. The vegetable desire to propagate dominates most people's lives to such an extent that they think of nothing else.

Generation after generation comes under this mating urge that has nothing to do with real choice. People may think that their relationship is unique but, except for a few outward differences, it is exactly like millions of others going on all over the world. This is the power of the Moon and the inferior planets of Mercury and Venus, not individual will.

The Moon, Mercury and Venus are the principles behind the vegetable processes within us. On the physical level the Moon governs the rhythms of organs and tissues and the inferior planets the monitoring mechanisms within the organism. Here, of course, the three can be seen in the operation of the astrological settings and their effect upon the biological functions. To illustrate this, let us suppose Venus is in its own sign of Taurus at the birth. This makes its influence very powerful in the body, thus making a considerable desire to encounter the pleasant and avoid the unpleasant. If Mercury, on the other hand, is in detriment in Pisces, then the body responses will be sluggish, the brain blurred and subject to periods of insensitivity and uncoordination. In the case of the Moon; if at birth it is found in, say, Sagittarius, then the organism will be inclined, if the Moon is badly aspected, to overspend its energy and waste its substance, thus the body will desire to move when it should rest and eat when it should diet. Here again we see how personal will has very little to do with how we act, in a bodily sense. The fact that we have these or those signs governing the Moon, Mercury and Venus has great relevance as to how we perform, not only in general but from day-to-day as the Moon shifts through the Zodiac. Thus on Monday, when it conjoins our natal Moon, we feel great and can start anything, while the following Monday when it is square to our natal Moon we feel low, despite having passed through a couple of days of flowing sextile. When the Moon comes into opposition to our natal Moon we are tense, having been through two days of relief in a Lunar trine, but this two-day tension is alleviated by another trine before we hit another day or two of squared difficulty prior to feeling like beginning the operation's next phase. Not much real initiative here if you are unaware of what is happening.

The body's state dominates most people because most people choose to 'live under the Moon,' as it is said. This means that they refuse or deny the option to rise above their physical condition. Here begins the first degree of choice. Now while the mineral, vegetable and animal kingdoms have no choice at all, because they are part of general evolution, mankind is not. Every human being has got the option of choice. That is his or her birthright. However, most people ignore this privilege and therefore relinquish the active rôle they can play in their own lives and in Creation. Now, some might argue that physical conditions preclude any decision about such sophisticated matters as free will but evidence does not back this up. Indeed, often in the most impoverished conditions, like in India, there are found the greatest exponents of spiritual matters and free will. Moreover, the reverse is often found in highly materially-advanced societies where people have leisure and a wide range of options. Free will is the right of all people and the first choice is to take it up or not. For those who avoid this right, it is not lost but placed in abeyance until Providence creates a crisis situation (which it usually does several times in each lifetime) for a decision to be made. This comes on the personal level or in a general situation like a national crisis that, for a period, shakes many people out of their Lunar habits. Indeed, it is said that this is the function of crisis and evil—but this will be discussed later. Those human beings who do take up the option of choice move on to the next degree; but this is still not truly free will for, while they may rise above the general law of vegetable and mineral conditioning, they are still subject to the desire of their animal aspect. The people who have reached this stage constitute the animal level of humanity.

The animal part of human nature is that aspect that has self-volition. This means that unlike a plant, which is basically static and influenced by its surroundings, the animal can manoeuvre. Taken on human vegetable and animal levels, the parallel is very precise. Whereas the vegetable state of man makes him passively subject to whatever is going on round him, the animal state is active in response. Seen astrologically, this means that a person begins to live off his Sun and not his Moon. That is, he has a degree of consciousness that the Lunar person has not and this gives him a completely different dimension and radius of action. In contrast to the vegetable person who more or less conforms to his environment and social customs, the animal person begins to assert individuality. He breaks and makes the rules, whereas the vegetable person merely perpetuates them because he chooses to do nothing else and therefore simply follows the old ways as they are the least trouble and afford the greatest security, no matter how bad or unjust they are. Anything is all right as long as one can survive without too much trouble, the Lunar-governed psyche thinks. Those governed principally by the Ascendant think even less and simply seek to meet the body's needs. The animal level rejects all this apparent lethargy and will-less-ness and desires to dominate the situation, then to change it to its own view.

The animal man and woman are easily recognised in any society. They are people of action. They stand out from the ordinary, not only by their bearing but by their vitality, be it the obvious Aries in its direct approach or the subtle but powerful diplomacy of the Libra, the cold, steel-chipping drive of the determined Virgo or the ambitious patience of the Capricorn's scheming. It can be perceived throughout all the signs, each one taking on the active aspect of its nature. There is not one that cannot express the power and volition of the animal level of a human being. The origin of this activity is decision. At some time in the person's existence they have chosen not to be passive as most people. They will not 'not do' as others. They will not be the servants of any situation because they see themselves as masters. This conclusion is quite different from the Lunar fantasy of the ego-Moon that just imagines it is master of itself

The animal person's confidence is based upon a glimpse of their possibilities, as embodied in their Sun sign wherein they perceive their real nature; what they were created for and what gifts and talents they possess. However, the vision, which perhaps came in childhood, youth or even in maturity, is partial because it initially creates only the desire to be different from others, to be superior to others. Such a view gives the kind of arrogance one would expect from the Solar principle that only sees its own glory. It would regard the world as its kingdom and that others should do its bidding because it could see, with the brilliant eye of the Sun, the truth about any situation. This sense of self-importance is the basis of most animal people's psychology and gives them the characteristic radiance that marks them out from the mass who follow their brilliance in whatever field they pursue their dominance.

It is in the nature of the animal kingdom to have a pecking order, a hierarchy of power, and so it is at the animal level of mankind. At first the young animal man makes his mark by being deliberately different from his fellows. In going his own way he often acquires followers over whom he exerts his desire to dominate. Every gang and social group has this phenomenon. It also occurs in political parties, fashionable society and many so-called religious communities. However, in the work and professional situation things are different because skills and precedents are involved. Ordinarily most people rise to position by virtuosity in their craft or trade or by the time-factor of seniority when they step into another's shoes. But in the animal man's case this is generally too slow or tiresome a process and so he either gets access to the top by making contact with the animal people then in power or by creating a crisis, even a revolution, to topple those holding the throne and so take over himself. This process is observed in great and small events, be it an office intrigue or *coup d'état*. Napoleon Bonaparte is the classic example of the animal man *par excellence*. Dramatic from the first, he stood out as a young artillery officer who, by manipulation, eliminated all other rivals. This element of conflict and confrontation is typical of the animal level, as might be expected. Astrologically, the animal man's Sun is the first stage of self-will. As such it overrides the reflective Lunar or ego level and dominates not only its own Moon but that of others who come within its rays. This radiance is the basis of the charismatic quality of animal people like Napoleon, who literally shine at any gathering of lesser Moon-governed people.

Now while Moon-dominated people have a life pattern, it is not so well defined as an animal person's fate. This is because the Lunar person is more subject to general external influences than the Solar person who follows his own nature. For example, a factory or office worker supporting his family, with no particular ambitions to fulfil his nature, is at the mercy of economic boom and recession and social changes. He cannot do anything about things as he sees it. All he wants is to be left to himself. Let others fight, strike and face the bosses or government. He will do nothing, except that of course when all his colleagues act *en masse* he will be right there with them, voting to strike, even if he thinks it is wrong, so strong is his need to conform. The animal man, on the other hand, might choose to lead the strike, or not to strike, because he has enough self-will to get out of a rut, as he sees it, into another kind of life. This manoeuvre is determined by his Solar principle which has shown him the truth of the matter. He then 'follows his star' which, as said, is an expression for being true to one's Sun. To be precise, the decision to move has been generated by the desire not to be thwarted from realising his possibilities. Whether he uses this animal drive for good or ill will be discussed later but he has, at this stage, without doubt acquired a degree of will. This characteristic we see in the leaders of every human-animal field. Ironically, without the animal or selfish determination of certain people there would be no progress, political or technical, because the mass of vegetable people would have remained in their caves until today, had they not been drawn or driven out by animal man's activities. Seen historically, the animal heroes and so-called villains of mankind have their place in the grand design of Creation. Attila the Hun's purging wars against the decadent Roman Empire were as necessary as the work of the self-centred astronomer Galileo in destroying the old, worn out, world picture held by medieval science.

It is an interesting fact to note, at this point, that people who do live off their Sun encounter more of their fate than those living off their Moon or Ascendant. By this is meant that they respond more fully to the astrological combinations in their horoscopes. Thus good and hard times, crises and changes have a deeper effect upon Sun-ruled people. None suffer so much as those who have strained and reached the heights and fallen in the depths. Ordinary vegetable people suffer but not to the same intensity, because their scale is less extreme and dramatic. That is why a real individual's life is usually richer but more traumatic than the person who just lives to survive. It is also the reason that the rewards and punishments of individual efforts are greater. For the animal man, desire and choice are what make his life interesting. However, as it should be appreciated by now, it is still a limited fate that he leads because, while he may dominate people with less will than himself, he is still at the mercy of his own bio-psychological desire to win and fear of defeat. He is imprisoned by his ambitions; locked in his fate until the victory or defeat of himself ceases to have any significance. This can only happen when the worship of himself becomes pointless and he awakens to something greater than the lowest manifestation of his Sun sign.

16. Sleeping and Awakening Suns

We have seen from the kabbalistic view how three Worlds meet in the Sun of an individual person, how the spirit underlays the psyche and how the body enclothes the two upper levels of reality within a man. Up until the last chapter we have examined the human situation on the premise that all people are at much the same natural level. Now we begin to differentiate between the natural and supernatural levels of human development. The first level, it has been shown, are those who live principally off their Ascendant, who care only for their survival and the pursuit of physical comfort. While one might find many such people everywhere, it should be noted that here also exists the criminal. One famous, or rather infamous, example is Gilles de Laval, known as Bluebeard, who raised money, so as to continue living in luxury, by sacrificing many people's lives in order to meet his side of a bargain with the Devil. As will be perceived, at this level there is no conscience and only enough of an acquired social code as to be just inside the law. There is only what the body craves for in creature comfort. Anything else is of no interest and others are merely seen as helpers or hinderers to physical security.

The second level is the ego-social and here we have seen how there is the compulsion to conform. The vast majority of the human race lives, to a greater or lesser degree, within this and the Ascendant level, going about their daily business of creating wealth, growing food, maintaining communications and supplying all the skills needed to run society in every country according to its cultural stage or political ideology. These two lower levels bring a person under the law of large numbers which subjects a person to the general fate of peoples as a national entity, like the USA going through its good and bad times. There is little true individuality here because people who live primarily off their Moons have been conditioned by their upbringing and society. Thus an Englishman has a certain set of outlooks which are quite different in flavour and emphasis from the Frenchman and even more so from the Chinese or Brazilian. Such bodily and cultural underlays are more powerful than is generally reckoned. When journeying

145

Figure 33 — DECISION
Here an animal man who has conquered the material World below recognises that all will be lost when he is displaced or dies. Suddenly there is an awful emptiness in his life when all his Earthly appetites have been satiated. Wealth, sex and power cannot bring permanent happiness or peace. He then begins to search out someone who has a truly fulfilled life. Here a spiritual teacher, symbolised by his wings, offers to take him up into the higher Worlds. The king of his world then has to choose what is really of value. (Alchemical woodcut, 17th century).

abroad it becomes soon very noticeable just how English one is—if you are English—in many things the ego-man considered as highly personal tastes and mannerisms. The national collective unconscious has a whole set of criteria by which we live that have nothing to do with our true natures. Living under one's Moon means that besides acting within our ethnic and Ascendant body-type, we mostly reflect what we have acquired. It is only those who live up to the third level of their Suns that have the beginning of originality and therefore individuality.

The animal man has the hallmark of individuality. He lives closer to his true nature than the Moon- and Ascendant-ruled people. This gives him a unique quality that is expressed in his life and fate. However, in most cases it only expresses the physical zenith of the Sun sign which is the lowest aspect of the Self. In such a condition a person may only dominate in the physical World and hold sway as long as his physical presence is there. We see this in commercial companies and political parties where, once the boss or leader has been removed, his influence quickly fades. This process is often accelerated by the next animal man to take over, who usually makes a clean sweep so as to assert his individual mark and power. It is interesting to note that often such people are self-made and that they frequently come from backgrounds of disadvantage or inferior position. For example, Hitler was an Austrian corporal, not of a German ruling class, while Disraeli, one of England's most brilliant Prime Ministers, had not one drop of white Anglo-Saxon Protestant blood in him. Here is the high impetus of desire which generates the powerful will to be accepted, then become the dominant head of a herd. This leads on to the fact that such achievement is in reality more of a compulsion, rather than a choice. Moreover, that this drive sometimes expresses the best and worst of a Sun sign. However, let us move on to begin to glimpse how the Sun can manifest physically, psychologically or spiritually. We will take three famous men to illustrate the Solar levels and confine them to Earth signs so as to perceive the difference between the quality of their Suns.

Mao Tse-tung, the founder of Communist China, came from a fairly modest background. With Sun in Capricorn and Moon in Leo he sought power with justice. After many setbacks and a slow hard ascent, he achieved unequalled ascendancy over his rivals and brought a pragmatic philosophy to his politics that gave the Chinese people their first firm and stable government for decades. As a practical man he spoke to the Chinese masses in their own terms and removed ancient decadences by implementing ruthless reforms. Here was the perfect blend of a Capricorn Sun and Leo Moon used at the physical and social levels.

Sigmund Freud, the psychologist, had his Sun in Taurus and Moon in Gemini. Sensual in Sun and intelligent in Moon, he probed into the psyche and detected the power of sex behind many of our drives. With Scorpio on the Ascendant, Moon in the 8th House and the Sun sign's ruling planet being Venus, it is not surprising that he perceived sex in everything. However, what is significant to us is the fact that he was using the second or psychological level of his Sun to perceive the world about him. Here the mixture of the two lower Worlds is well illustrated but not the third of the Spirit—for Freud considered matters of Spirit and Divine as deep psycho-sensual needs and projections.

Sir Isaac Newton was a Sun Capricorn and Moon Cancer. He was, however, more than a practical thinker. His observations about a falling apple and his conclusions that everything affected everything else were the perception of a visionary rather than a strict scientist. Indeed he saw the visible and the invisible Universe as a single whole and his generally unknown writings on the Bible and its inner meaning indicate a cosmic and spiritual outlook. Here is a perfect example of an individual reversing the common view that a Sun and Moon opposition is bad. The Moon in his 9th House of wisdom acts as a deep reflector to the Sun in the study House of the 3rd and his Libra Ascendant has been converted into a truly liberal and balanced view of physical reality. It was Newton who rebuked Halley on deriding astrology with the throwaway line: 'The difference between you and I is that I have studied it and you have not!' For such width and depth of scale to be found in so fastidious a scientist is the hallmark of the third and spiritual level of the Sun. Newton, in spite of his practical and social skills, showed that he could transcend not just space in his study but time, in that much of his work is still valid while the work of Mao and Freud has already dated.

The Sun, it will be remembered, is at the top of the physical Tree, at the centre of the psychological Tree and at the base of the Tree of the Spirit. At the centre of the planetary or subtle body it is the focus of incoming and outgoing influence. In the person governed principally by the Ascendant or Moon it constitutes an unseen watcher which, in moments of extraordinary crisis or peace, may emerge out of the unconscious to speak or show some truth about the person or their situation. In the case of the animal person, he or she is dimly aware of the inner Sun and carries its directions out in a physical and practical way because they do not know, and often do not care, about the psychological, let alone the spiritual implications of its direction. In modern times, since the discoveries of Freud and Jung, the psychological aspect of man, to the Western world, has become more and more important, not only because it explains so many personal problems and reasons for social and antisocial behaviour but because the orthodox Western spiritual traditions have lost their insight and knowledge of such matters in their descent into mere outer ritual and social issues. With this desire for understanding the nature of the psyche comes a response in the many psychological workshops throughout the Western world and in the springing up of spiritual movements since the 1960s. Providence always answers such a need because it is concerned with mankind's development. This need to grow as a person and relate to the world is now to be found everywhere and, indeed, it brings many people together who normally would never meet. There are, at the present time, more traditions and techniques available than at any other period of history. Some of these are complete teachings; others are not only incomplete but also garbled versions of the nature of man and the Universe. The phenomenon of distorted instruction and misdirection is one of the problems that the seeker after knowledge has to resolve as he or she trudges from one guru to another to find out which one makes sense to his or her temperament and type. The exercise of trying this and that method, however, is in no way a waste but the first test of discrimination in the journey of the soul. Here we come to a major point. Until now we have studied the three levels of ordinary life. Now begins the rise above ordinary terrestrial natural law and into the supernatural sphere of the awakening soul. This grants a kind of freedom unknown to what are called 'the sleeping members of mankind.'

There is an ancient myth that says that the goddess of the Moon was the offspring of the union between the goddess of the Earth and the god of the Sun; and that this Moon goddess was the love object of the god of Nature. However, the Moon goddess loved Endymion who had been placed in a state of sleep so that she could visit and speak to him in his dreams. The symbolic meaning of this tale becomes apparent when we reflect on the general state of mankind, living under the rulership of the Ascendant of the Earth and the Moon. It tells us, for example, that the power of the Moon works through the unconscious of people as she holds them in dreams and habits. The Moon's interest in mankind is greater than in Nature, because man is the spearhead of development on the Earth and, as such, is capable of a wider and deeper spectrum of consciousness than any other species of animal or plant. However, because the human race is the progeny of the heavens as well as the Earth, its potential to rise above the level of the physical World is realisable, as against Nature which is strictly earthbound. Here we have the crucial difference, not only between Nature and mankind but between people who wish to awaken and people who desire only to continue sleeping in the arms of the Earth Ascendant and under the Moon. At the present time the Solar system is entering a new phase and mankind is stirring in its slumber. This happens from time to time in great movements and activities, such as the period around 500 BC when many people, all over the known world from China to Greece, were awakened to the cosmic and spiritual aspects of Creation. We are now, early in the twenty-first century, at another such time. That is why there is such interest in things spiritual and psychological and why the knowledge of such matters, hidden for so long, is coming into the open.

How, one might ask, does this relate to the individual? Another myth, one of Plato's, gives a hint as it explains man's natural condition—I repeat 'natural' condition. In this allegory some people are in a cave, behind them is a fire which throws their shadows on the cave wall. Most of the people see these flickering projections and imagine this is real life and that the ever-moving shadow figures is where the action is because they cannot see themselves, so fascinated are they by the images projected by something behind their (physical) consciousness. One man, however, manages to turn and see the fire and, recognising that the shadows are an illusion, stumbles away from the fascination of the fire (the psychological Sun) to the entrance of the cave where he discovers daylight. On coming out of the cave he is, for a while, blinded by the intensity of the (spiritual) Sun, then his vision clears and he perceives a magnificent (cosmic) landscape before him. It is quite unlike the limited world of the cave with its groping and shadowy reality. This is so obviously the real world that he decides to return and tell his fellows about it. Going back into the dark cave, he makes his way to the entranced crowd as they watch the flickering shadows play. However, despite his story of the upper world, they will not listen to him and reject his description as fantasy and him as mad. This is the situation of the supernatural man in relation to the natural man.

What does it mean to be a supernatural man or woman? It means to be above nature, to rise above natural law. This is not a process that takes place overnight. It is a long drawn-out journey, often over many lives but it can be accomplished, we are told, if enough will is there, in a single lifetime. The first stage is to recognise one's actual situation and this usually occurs in those moments when we come out of the preoccupations of the Ascendant and the illusions of the Moon-ego and into the first state of the Sun. This means we glimpse what we are, what our body-type is, how our ego can be converted from a little tin god into a useful servant to reflect the truth of the Sun. Now here, as noted, is the temptation to believe that we have arrived because we have attained a degree of Sun-consciousness and self-will. This might make us a hero, as the Greeks called such a person, as against a common man; however, even heroes can be fools and are destroyed by their fate. The next step is to still pass through one's fate—because that is largely unavoidable—but be inwardly unaffected by it, that is, not be dependent on it. When Napoleon, for example, was exiled to an Atlantic island remote from his field of glory he collapsed as a man. So, too, did Mussolini when fate reversed his fortunes—as it must, by astrological law, from time to time. The individual who can pass through success and failure with sublime indifference is master of his fate. This can only be done by real knowledge, not by deliberate ignorance.

The kind of knowledge termed here is not the Mercurial type of information and fact but that born of inner experience, by wisdom and understanding of the real nature of oneself and one's place in the Universe. This is the knowledge spoken of at the beginning of this book and it starts to be acquired with the awakening out of the Ascendant and Lunar states to the self. Seen kabbalistically it is the shift of emphasis out of the influence of the physical World into the World perceived by the psychological Sun. This is astrologically accomplished by observing and controlling the power of the Ascendant and the Moon-ego and watching over the principles of Mercury and Venus as these inferior planets create moods according to their positions and relationships in the macrocosm. The next step is to study the Zodiacal nature of one's Sun and its aspects to the superior planets and so gain a working knowledge of the contents of one's particular psyche and its balances and tendencies. Here is where the horoscope set out on the Tree diagram becomes real to the Kabbalist as a working method of psychological and spiritual evolution.

17. The Psyche and Its Contents

It can be said that the composition of the psyche is divided into three broad areas. The first and lowest is the ordinary consciousness of a person. Here is the mind used in everyday life to handle the affairs of the physical world as they come into contact with the subtle body. The second is that part of the psyche that lies just beyond the ordinary threshold of consciousness and influences the person, often unbeknown to him. This is the emotional part of the subtle body and, in moments of wakefulness, it is the arbiter of conscience and insight. It also acts as the intermediary between the ego level of ordinary mind and the third and deeper level of the true unconscious which contains many things, both ancient and current, of which the person is totally unaware and yet is profoundly moved by all his life—and, indeed, all his incarnated lives.

Set out astrologically on the kabbalistic Tree of the Psyche, the first level is made up of the Ascendant, the Moon, Mercury and Venus. These form a geometric triangle with the Moon-ego at the centre of three small triads. This arrangement not only shows the active and passive roles of Venus and Mercury but the interaction of the Moon and Ascendant with them to create a threefold mechanism that brings them all into relationship. Firstly, as said, the Ascendant gives a form to the ethnic and family body inherited by an individual with the Zodiacal sign and its ruler, and any planets found in the 1st House, setting a particular cast of physical quality. Likewise, the type of ego is affected by the sign the Moon occupies and is afflicted or enhanced by any aspects to that luminary. The qualitative factor also applies to the Mercurial and Venusian principles and the signs they occupy, plus their aspects. All this forms a unique combination which is expressed in the great Mercury-Venus-Ascendant triangle of the bio-psychological mechanism.

Now the three small triads composed by the inferior planets, Moon and Ascendant are the thinking, feeling and doing parts of the ordinary mind. The thinking process is essentially a passive or reflective function and so we find it composed of Mercury, the Moon and the Ascendant.

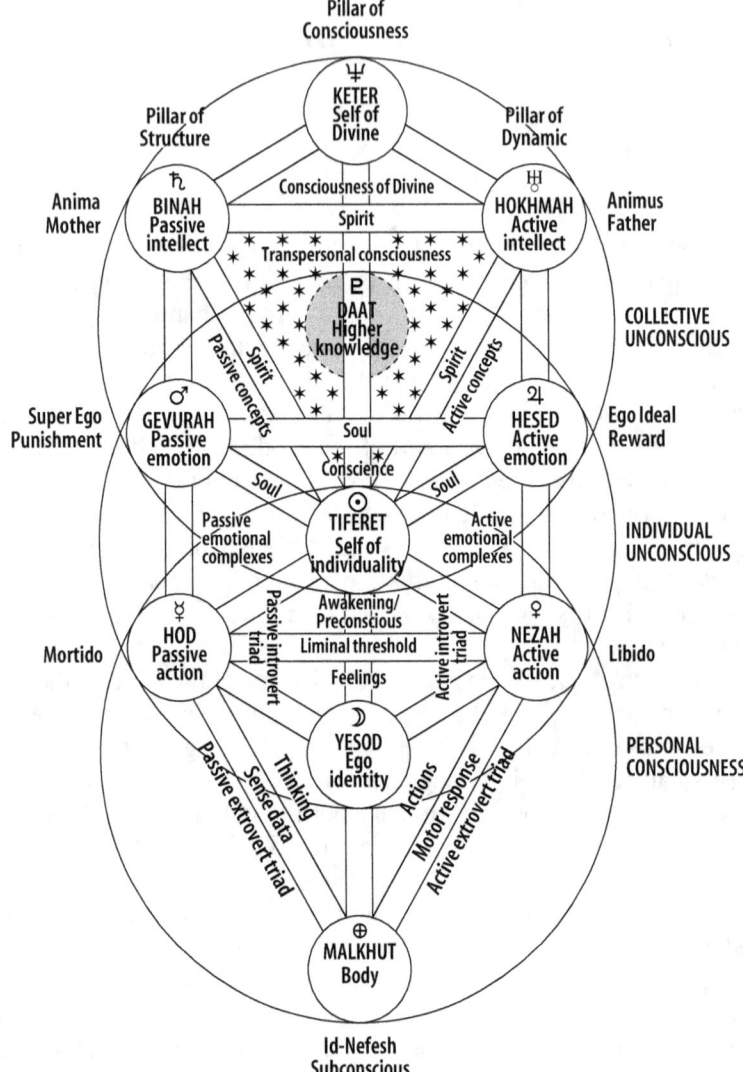

Figure 34—CONTENTS OF THE MIND
The psyche is a very complex organism. It has, besides its dynamic and structure, seven degrees of consciousness, various functions, loadings and emphases, according to one's body type, conditioning and astrological configurations. Besides whether one is an Earthy, Watery, Airy or Fiery person, there are the memories of this life and those before, as well as the patterns of the present culture. All these have to be co-ordinated by the Sun of the Self and the outer planets of the unconscious. Only the soul triad of Mars, Jupiter and the Sun can change things through an act of free will. (Halevi).

It is that part of the mind which figures out ordinary mental problems according to previous data or experience stored in the unconscious. It is not intellectual contemplation, although its cleverness and remarkable memory might sometimes be mistaken by the unperceptive as such. A good librarian is not the same as a bad but real thinker. The second small triad, composed of the Ascendant, the Moon and Venus, is called the triad of action. This is because the function generated by being on the active side of the complex is concerned with those biopsychological processes which relate the Venusian desire for movement and the ego's connection with the body through the Ascendant. Here is where the ordinary mind implements the thoughts and solutions worked out by the thinking triad. It makes the body do this or that, sometimes acting from the ego and sometimes influenced from beyond the threshold of consciousness. The third triad, called the 'feeling' function, is composed of Mercury, Venus and the Moon. Here it will be observed that there is no direct connection with the Ascendant. This makes for a detached and volatile area of the mind having no physical links, except through the ego-Moon, with the Ascendant which is the mind's connection to the body. The feeling-type function arises because of its association with both side pillars which makes it highly susceptible to active and passive fluctuation. As the feeling part of the ego it is the mood maker in the lower part of the psyche.

In the ideal, the functions of thinking, feeling and action are equally balanced in a person. This, we know, is impossible for ordinary man; partly because he has little or no knowledge of, or control over, his mind but also because of the particular astrological tensions created by the zodiacal relationships of the Ascendant, Moon, Mercury and Venus in any given horoscope. Thus, for example, because Mercury is in its own sign of Virgo and Venus is in detriment in Scorpio, the balance will be more of the reflective and inactive kind, thus making the thinking function predominate. Conversely, suppose the reverse was the case with Venus well aspected while Mercury was afflicted. This would encourage the triad of action and produce a doer rather than a thinker. Whether for good or bad purpose is another matter, because here we are speaking of function, not conscience. In a like manner, the sign of the Moon will affect the balance of the triads. Supposing the Moon was in Aquarius which is an active Fixed sign. The result would be, with say Venus also in this sign, more inclined to the action triad but with a difference because, being an Air sign, the initiative would be of a mental nature, stimulating and yet inherently Fixed, active but not practical. Thus the oscillation between revolution and fear of change, so characteristic of Moon Aquarians, would place its mark on the lower mind. Again in contrast, supposing the Moon were in Libra. Here the triad emphasised would be the action one because of the Venus rulership and the Cardinal desire to do something; while Moon in Scorpio would encourage, because of its Fixed, Watery secretiveness, an inclination to emphasise the feeling triad with a dogmatic quality in all its moods. For similar but physical reasons, the signs and planets in the Ascendant would also make their contribution to the emphasis of the precedence in the thinking, feeling and doing triads.

All the foregoing lays out the setting of the lower psyche. These emphases indicate the way we receive the incoming of data from the outside world and implement the outgoing dictates of the psyche. With a little observation or examination of one's chart, one should soon be able to see whether one begins any enterprise or responds to a situation by thinking, feeling or wishing to act first. This knowledge is the first major step in commanding oneself. Without the consciousness of how one reacts to exterior or interior situations, any comprehension of the middle and deep psyche is just theory.

The triad composed of Mercury, Venus and the Sun is that area of the lower mind that lies just beyond everyday ego-consciousness. It is, however, the level we attain when occasionally we awake during a crisis or a moment of deep peace or happiness. This is because we have passed through the veil of the threshold between Mercury and Venus and out of the ordinary functions and processes of the ego mind to experience direct contact with ourselves as expressed in the Sun. Such moments or periods are generated by Grace from deep in the psyche or by the result of hard work on controlling the processes of the ordinary body-mind. Either way there is a sense of illumination and lucidity in which the lower part of oneself is observed with a clarity and knowledge, unfortunately often to be forgotten when the attention slips into the ego state again, such is the habitual power of the inferior planets, Moon and Ascendant. However, experience of this awakening triad gives us access to the middle part of the psyche, composed of Mercury, Mars and Saturn on the passive side and Venus, Jupiter and Uranus on the active side, with the Sun as central pivot on the middle column.

As will be seen, the above complex creates on the Tree a set of four small triads attached to the side columns. The lower two, made up of Mars and Mercury and Jupiter and Venus, which are all centred on the Sun, are the storehouse of emotional memories and complexes. Those stored on the left are concerned with the conservative aspect of our emotional lives: the fears, resistances, love of form, need for support and memories that guard, hold and constrain our emotional lives. In the right-hand triad of Venus, Sun and Jupiter is to be found the need to love, initiate, create, forgive and explore. Here are stored all the emotional memories that make us affirm life, hope and ever extend our openness and vulnerability. These emotional complexes are quite different from day-to-day moods of the feeling triad below. They are concerned with the whole lifetime and influence most people unconsciously by permeating ego consciousness with basic attitudes of reserve or outgoingness, deep-seated fear or optimism. One can feel very upset over buying the wrong pair of shoes but this is not on the same scale as being profoundly depressed about constant professional failure. Nor is the ephemeral pleasure of sexual success the same as the deep pleasure of a lasting relationship. These inner triads represent, for most of us, the unconscious emotional climate of our lives and their balance, needless to say, is also governed by the astrological settings of the superior planets and the Sun.

To illustrate this, let us take one or two examples. Supposing a person has Mars in the passive sign of Virgo. This planet, being in a debilitating sign, will constrict the emotional power of Mars even more than its natural inclination to a tight emotional discipline. Thus the person's emotional memories and subsequent associations that form into psychological complexes will be flavoured by a highly critical, judging and narrow outlook unless it is alleviated by a good aspect from the emotionally expansive planet Jupiter. In a like manner, supposing Mars was in its own sign of Aries. This would create a less conservative flavour among the passive emotional complexes and the way in which the memories were arranged, so that any unpleasant events would be forgotten or at least diminished in interest once the issue was in the past, whereas Mars in Capricorn would harden their substance and tighten the knot until the matter had been resolved in revenge or justice many years later unless, again, relieved by the good aspect of Jupiter. Looking at the active side of the emotional triads, the position of Jupiter is just as critical. If, say, a planet is deposited in Pisces then an excess of emotional openness is to be expected while, if Jupiter is placed in, say, Gemini, in which it is in detriment, a certain scattering, indiscrimination and forgetfulness of emotional lessons learned might be expected. However, if Jupiter is in Cancer a certain controlled generosity to the person's own kin and circle will manifest in loving memories, acts of largesse and mercy. A similar emotional attitude might be found in one with Jupiter in Aries where a massive desire to please could lead to an occasional emotional excess and possible indiscretion. As will be seen, the placings and aspects to the other planets are crucial and affect the kind of things stored or rejected by the emotional memory banks of the unconscious.

The intellectual storehouse in the triads composed, on the passive side, by Mars, Saturn and the Sun, and Jupiter, Uranus and the Sun on the active, operate on exactly the same principles as the emotional triads except that these are the ideas and concepts taken in during the early life and subsequently modified by experiences. As such these have a very deep effect on the psyche of a person. For example, here are stored all the traditions of one's family, people and philosophy, be it Christian, Buddhist or Communist. Imbibed in childhood and youth the ideas embedded are, for most people, very rarely changed despite the apparent transformations going on outside. The lapsed Catholic, when the crunch comes, still refers to his church's view even if he rejects it. The dissident Jew cannot quite get rid of four thousand years of history and the Chinese in Communist China is still either a Confucian or Taoist at heart. Indeed, Mao Tse-tung recognised this inherent set of Chinese concepts and modified European Communism to suit the Chinese mind.

Such concepts are very deep-set and can only be changed by profound revelation which tells us that, for most people, only the passive or formal side of our concepts, ruled principally by Saturn, is operative. Here we see the accumulation of experience over the years slowly harden into a set of formal concepts and traditions. Here emerges the classic Saturnine attitude, unless it is offset by Saturn being in a more radical sign like Aries which would make the intellect continually test well-tried principles if it were well aspected. A different kind of conflict or modification would occur among the passive concepts of a person if Saturn were placed in Sagittarius. This would also defuse the rigidity of ideas but be more soft in its approach to conservative attitudes. The converse would occur if the planet were in Capricorn which would produce a strictly orthodox outlook of concepts unless, again, benevolently aspected by Jupiter or Venus. Uranus in the various signs would have its illuminating but erratic

THE PSYCHE AND ITS CONTENTS 157

effects upon the active or revelationary ideas of a person. Thus one would have original but disciplined thinking if the planet were found in Virgo, while Uranus in Aries would produce some remarkable but foolhardy inventions alongside many innovative schemes. The contents of this active triad of intellect would be disturbed or stabilised depending on any aspects made to Uranus. While all have occasional flashes of genius, some experience periodic bursts of illumination. This often happens to those people who have Uranus in its own sign of Aquarius. They live in a different world from the rest of us mortals. Such people range from the visionaries, the brilliant philosophers and the genius inventors to being diabolic crooks and insane prophets. The modification and emphasis of the planets, signs and aspects is, of course, affected by the particular House in which they are placed. The interaction with the mundane is the outward manifestation of the emotional and intellectual triads. The particular configuration of complexes and concepts, when set at the moment of birth, forms the hidden guide-rails of fate.

The function of the Sun is to act as the focus to the intellectual planets, the emotional planets and the inferior planets and Moon of the lower mind which, in the kabbalistic scheme, interleaves through the Ascendant with the Tree of the Body. The Sun is the essence of a person, the three-fold Self that lies at the centre of his being. It is, it will be recalled, the apex of the body's consciousness and the centre of the subtle anatomy. As the latter, it is the psychological pivot of the individual and acts as the co-ordinator to all the associated planetary principles and their particular astrological settings. The implication of this is vitally significant because, while the planetary functions, Moon and Ascendant have influence and power, none have so crucial a position in the individual as the Sun has. This is why the Sun sign is so important in the horoscope. The Sun, be it the conscious or unconscious director of the life, is the Seat of Solomon, as it is called in Kabbalah, of the person.

Seen strictly at the psychological level, the Sun is the junction of all the incomings and outgoings in the psyche. All the triads of intellect and emotion meet here; so too does the Mercury-Sun-Venus triad of awakening which is the highest level of physical awareness. With the transformation of the physical Sun to the psychological Sun, the planetary weightings begin to manifest more fully instead of merely being a background influence. Thus the person who lives off his psychological Sun has, even if he is relatively unconscious of them, to contend with the strengths and weaknesses within the subtle body as it works more directly through the emotional and intellectual triads to affect his life. This is when the mechanism of fate really begins to operate as the mundane Houses express materially the contents of the planetary body as its character, free of the physical constraints, starts to assert itself. For example, if Mars is in Virgo in the 10th House, all the ideas and emotions associated with the Mars-Virgo combination will filter through to affect the professional direction and ambitions of the man attracting him, for example, to medicine or accountancy. In contrast, supposing a well-aspected Venus in Leo is found in the 2nd House, the practical, stylish and active desire to acquire beautiful things might well show itself in a gift for fashionable interior decorating, collecting and selling *objets d'art* or dress design. This particular life would, unless there were overridingly bad aspects elsewhere, certainly be oriented towards tasteful comfort, if not luxury. From just these two examples can be seen how the balance of all the factors in the Tree of the horoscope, operating through the Houses, will determine the quality and characteristic of the life lived. In other words, the form of the fate. In many quite intelligent individuals this process is, for the most part, fairly unconscious because they are only living off the middle and lower part of the psyche, thus it is still a question of degree of knowledge and choice.

Here again it must be repeated, because it is so easily forgotten, that partial knowledge is not enough for, although a person may live what appears to be a very distinct kind of life, it is often, in fact, only the mechanical result of the psychological loading of a horoscope. This means that while an individual may override physical difficulties, he may be still subject to a set of internal psychological or planetary pressures that compel him to act out a preset pattern. Thus, while such gifted, remarkable and intelligent persons may seem to escape the general mass law that affects most of mankind, they are, in fact, held fast within the psychological realm and dominated by the current planetary conditions and, therefore, not masters of their lives. In order to rise above the subtle domination of fate which can cast one down as well as raise one up, the next step is to see consciously into the depths of the psyche and come to know its strengths and weaknesses so as to begin to govern one's fate. This means to convert the unconscious into the conscious, to take over from the automatic pilot of inevitability and at least control the interior responses to outer events that must still occur. Such a step requires the deliberate operation of the triad Sun-Mars-Jupiter which, as said, is called in Kabbalah the soul or the place of Self-consciousness. Here begins the work to detach oneself from one's fate while having to live through its outward pattern. As Shakespeare wrote: 'The fault, dear Brutus, is not in our stars, but in ourselves; that we are underlings.' Esoteric teaching takes it further in saying 'one must die to this World while still living.'

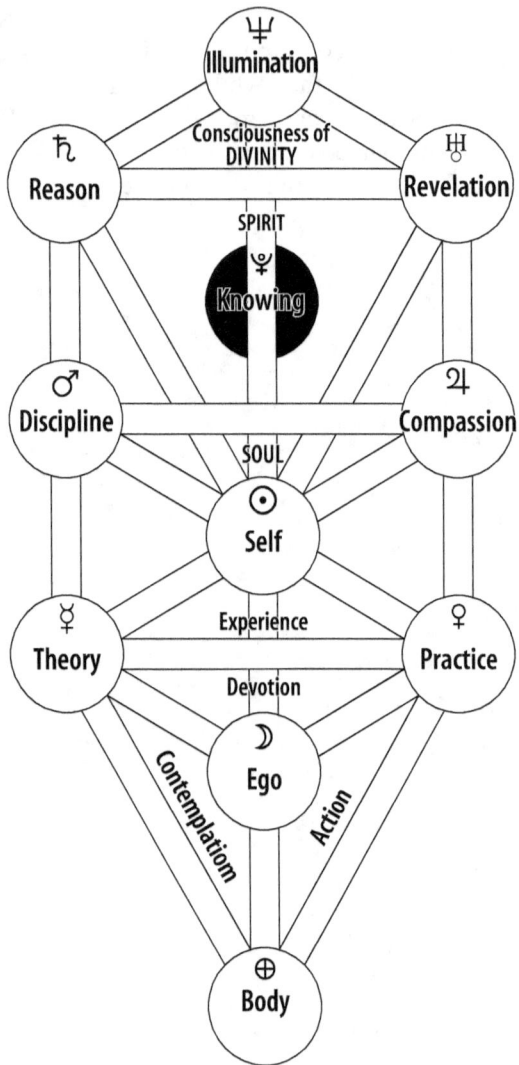

Figure 35 — METHOD
In order to discover what one's fate is, it is necessary to apply a working method. One may be very familiar with one's birth chart but most people have a passive attitude which means that they do nothing with their knowledge. In this Tree, one uses the Sun, Moon and planets as instruments whereby one may exploit the possibilities seen in the birth chart and reduce the negatives. One can use Mars as a principle of discipline or Jupiter to open out opportunities. A Saturn or Uranus transit can be a time to plan long-term or revolutionise one's life. Fate may be fixed but the lesson is to build on it. (Halevi).

18. The Soul

Sir Thomas Browne, a seventeenth-century English physician, wrote: 'Burden not the back of Aries, Leo or Taurus with thy faults, nor make Saturn, Mars or Venus guilty of thy follies. Think not to conceive thyself under a fatality of being evil. Calculate thyself within. Seek not thyself in the Moon, but in thine own orb or microcosmical circumference.' In this quotation is the notion of freedom from fate. But before we speak of freedom from fate, let us understand yet more precisely what fate is.

By identifying the tendencies in a chart it is possible to recognise that a certain kind of temperament will generate a certain type of life pattern. Thus, for example, a man with, say, an afflicted Mars in Aries in the 1st House, in conjunction with Uranus which is also afflicted, will have the effect of producing a rather impulsive and occasionally violent person. The result of this is that he will create confrontational situations in which he will continually react irrationally. Such a person finds little peace and will, as one astrologer said of this condition, 'Seek continual crisis as a way of life.' Conversely someone with Sun and Moon in Pisces in the 12th House will endlessly look to retire, to hide and live in his own private world, and this will result in the life of a recluse, if there is enough wealth to avoid work, or a profession where the person works at home or in some place tucked away from the mainstream of life, like a bookworm scholar, writer, painter or monk. From these two examples it can be seen that the pattern of the lives are to a degree predetermined, in that a person's nature creates a life style that is then fixed into a habitual set of reflexes. If one considers how difficult it is to change a recognisable habit like smoking or walking in a certain way, one can see how almost impossible it is to change undetected psychological habits.

This observation about known and unknown habits reveals just how the tendency of fate is reinforced and becomes almost rigid. However, this inflexibility has its purpose in that our fatal patterns fit into the lives of others about us. Indeed, it was designed by Providence into a local external situation with these others in order to work out some problems and improve the performance of our being. Thus it is that while we are unable to manage our own affairs consciously, the macrocosm creates just the right circumstances to aid our perfection, although while involved in the suffering we do not always appreciate the lesson at the time. The implication of all this is that there is a preordained element in our lives that cannot be altered. This is true but only to a matter of degree. For those who live principally in the physical and lower psychological Worlds, life is indeed fixed by external events and habits. But with the beginning of Self-consciousness or the awareness of one's psychological makeup, through a discipline like Kabbalah or, as in this case, practical astrology, there begins the exercise of will.

Up till now we have seen how little will there is in most people. They either conform to the demands of the body, the social pressure of society or the conditioning of the ego. They are, in fact, will-less or will-full depending upon whether they are subject to the passive or active aspects of these lower levels. With the beginning of a psychological Self-awareness comes a willingness that is an acknowledgement of something greater than anything offered by the mineral, vegetable or animal levels of human existence. This willingness means submission to a higher influence and authority within. The outer manifestation here is often in the seeking of a guru or spiritual teacher. While this is initially necessary, the true significance is that the person is turning to and placing himself under the tutelage of the soul.

The soul is the heart of the psyche. It is that factor in the subtle anatomy that hovers between the physical body below and the spirit above. It is part of the psyche and yet not directly involved with the various mental mechanics of the ego's consciousness or the various triads of emotional complexes and intellectual concepts. Set out diagrammatically on the Tree of the psyche, it will be recalled that it is composed of the triad cornered by Mars, Jupiter and the Sun. As such it has a distinctly emotional character. However, there is a major difference. Situated where it is on the central column, it is concerned with matters of consciousness and will. This means that, quite unlike the side or lower triads, it has a conscious rather than functional power. An example of this is that while an emotional memory may be very potent, it cannot bring about change. It can only be repeated on recall, whereas any event occurring in the soul triad of Self-consciousness, like remorse, can precipitate change. That is why this triangle is sometimes called the Place of Conscience.

The Soul

In traditional terms, the soul triad is the place where purification occurs; it is also the area where purgatory is experienced as the good and bad elements stored in the emotional and intellectual side triads are brought before the eye of the soul in a moment of Self-consciousness. Here we see the full psychological action of the Sun whose symbol is Apollo, the god of Truth. It is said that few can meet Apollo's blinding eye or avoid his unerring arrows of truth that strike home and deep into the heart of any matter. Apollo also has, myth reports, a remarkable harp which can bring such harmony that even wild beasts will dwell in peace with those they attack. Seen psychologically, this is the harmonising aspect of the Seat of Solomon that brings co-ordination and law to the warring factions of the body and psyche. The planets Mars and Jupiter, as aspects of the soul, operate as the Justice and Mercy principles that sit in watch over the moments of Self-awareness. They reveal to the psychological Self the evil and good and judge and forgive in order to bring about equilibrium. If there were only a Martial aspect to the combination then the psyche would be unbalanced, hard and puritan to a fault in its strictness and only astringent in its actions. Likewise, if there were only the Jovian principle in operation there would only be a forever-forgiving tolerance that would allow bad habits to be perpetuated and grow into evil manifestations for which the psyche and the body would have to pay dearly. Mars and Jupiter, however, not only check and counterbalance each other but act as the controlling and expansive factors in the person's psychological life. This process is usually not observed in everyday events but goes on unconsciously building up or holding back, behind the small happenings, an accelerating progression that usually surfaces only during a major life crisis where a curtailment or an expansion of some important issue must be taken. It is at such moments that most people wake up psychologically and have to make a conscious choice, whether they like it or not. One can never say that one has not the birthright of free will.

Let us take an example of such a moment of choice. Supposing a man has Mars transiting his natal Mars in his 7th House of partners and it is in the sign of, say, Libra, where it is in detriment. The situation produced by the combination would be to precipitate a major decision about a partner, say his wife, and their relationship. Being in Libra, the choice of options would not be easy. The chances are, with this astrological set-up, that the decision to marry was not a wise one but rather a formal partnership that had either been drifted into, because of the indecisiveness of the man in the face of a pleasant compromise, or one of sudden impulse when the decision was no doubt forced by his desire, or his future wife's, for some or any kind of action. Let us now suppose that the results of that decision have come full circle, perhaps the result of the Mars return two years later or the eighteen-year cycle of the Moon, which comes into the same combination with the Sun as the day the decision or marriage was made, or a Saturn return which is transiting its original position in the horoscope of the relationship. The nature and depth of the crisis would be determined by these factors and other planetary aspects.

The man, in the case of a Mars transit, at first senses, then feels, then thinks that something is wrong as the Mars conjunction approaches, according to his thinking, feeling or acting type. He would then replay many memories from his emotional and intellectual stores in the unconscious about the situation prior to the marriage and the immediate post-marriage period. Such an operation would produce in him much tension and this, in turn, would be communicated to his wife who, of course, would respond because they must be related astrologically in some way or they would not be married.

The crunch proper would begin as Mars entered fully into the relevant sign and House. Its psychological effect would be to increase the tension in the unspoken moods and preoccupation. It would further heighten as the orb of Mars touched the outer orb, of about two degrees, of the natal Mars. At this point the problem that had, up till now, been put off would confront the couple. Either he or she, in response to the constriction of Mars and its sense of justice or injustice, would break the tension and bring the issue into the open. If the man were what is called an inferior man, that is governed by his Ascendant, Moon or physical Sun, the result would be either a violent outburst of undisciplined emotion or an over-controlled repression of the truth about the situation as he sought, in Libran compromise, to comfort himself and avoid the problems of the relationship. If this latter position were to be held and maintained by the wife then the marriage would continue, after a fashion, in a partnership of convenience and lies because the opportunity for integrity, given by Mars, would be lost. If the confrontation alternative occurred then it could either break the marriage up or, after a short outburst, swing back into habit because of the coward-producing detriment of Mars in Libra, and continue as a placating compromise again. In all cases, once the conjunction was over and the decision taken (and even a non-decision is a decision), then the die is cast for the next two years. All this is supposing that the husband and wife have no Self-consciousness, except for the fact that, at the crunch point of the conjunction, both are dimly aware that it is a fatal decision—to break or continue an unbalanced situation. Such is the power of habit that few inferior men or women do anything. They relinquish the possibility of free will and so remain locked in fate until external circumstance precipitates another crisis.

In the case of what is called a superior man or woman the situation is quite different. While the external events might be just the same and indeed all the moods and replaying of memory records identical, the handling of the circumstance would be perceived from a deeper point of view. Firstly he, if we take the husband, would see the situation as a learning one. He would realise, even if he was unaware of the Mars conjunct Mars—for not all people trying to evolve themselves are astrologers—that an important moment was imminent. He would, however, view the partnership (and even his bad choice in a moment of passion) as an event in which he could come to know more about his weaknesses, strengths and yet more truth about his own nature. By taking a vantage point from the soul triad of Self-consciousness he would be, as Shakespeare's Polonius advised, true to 'thine own self' and therefore unable to be false unto any man or woman. This basis is the only one for any improvement in the marriage if it is to continue. Such a relatively objective vision of his own temperamental composition would give him insights into his wife's inner character and the real significance of their fatal relationship, no matter how superficially bad it appeared. He would, for example, be able to recognise, perhaps, his desire for a mother figure or a daughter substitute, so that he could avoid the responsibility of meeting a woman on equal terms as an adult peer. He might, in another case, perceive how his wife brought out the worst side of, for instance, his indecision, in that she took all the initiatives. At such a moment of truth he could, with conscious will, resolve the situation and decide to change the *status quo,* first in himself and then the relationship. If his wife objected, he might have to fight, another Martial talent, for his integrity. There are many situations and combinations in which this might show up. However, if he did consciously decide to take action then the future could, unless he reverted to an inferior status, well change for the good the interior and subsequently the exterior aspect of the relationship, be it towards greater intimacy or a correctly carried out separation.

Figure 36—EXPANSION
Here the astrologer, Kabbalist or practioner of whatever esoteric tradition he may follow, breaks through the bonds of physical perception to see the processes that govern fate. With such knowledge he may make preparation for hard times, exploit favourable transits and become master of his fate. This leads on to what his destiny might be, for to know who and what you are is the key to what your mission might be, not only in this life but in the past and future. Wise individuals remember and practise in this incarnation for what is to come. (16th century woodcut).

As will be perceived, such an event would reveal much about a person and all those emotionally connected with him because every one of a person's family, friends and even professional advisers would be affected, to a greater or lesser degree, by what happened in such a crisis. In this way one begins to see how various lives and fates are interwoven. The implication is enormous. Firstly, besides the Self-knowledge gained by such happenings, there is a slight alteration in the balance of a particular circle of people. One only has to witness the divorce and breakup of a family to realise that its effect is far beyond the local home and hearth. This alteration can be seen as a shift in a social situation where people simply rearrange themselves in new partnerships and repeat their fatal patterns; or the change can be an actual attempt to learn and grow out of the old and confining habits. While this is rare amongst those who crave vegetable comfort or desire to be the dominant animal, it is not uncommon amongst those who would seek to be truly human. Humanness is a quality of the soul. This is because the soul contains the discretion of a refined and gentle Mars and the compassion of a disciplined Jupiter in combination with an honest but clement Sun. This matured state can only be the result of conscious work.

Conscious work is the hallmark of the superior man and woman. It means perceiving what is really going on in a situation and recognising not only others' unconscious motivations, but one's own—that is, making the unconscious conscious. It then means that one takes on the responsibility for one's interior and exterior actions, cultivating the useful and good and curtailing the useless and bad. This is an occupation that is worked at every second, minute and hour of the day and night, year in and year out. Any lapses often result in expensive loss because the gains that most people are ordinarily unaware of are quickly lost and what would be a trivial mistake for an inferior man is not seen in the same way by one working on his soul. For example, it is common for people to take what are considered rightful perks from their place of work. A person trying to be a human, instead of a vegetable or animal man, cannot do this because it is, in plain terms, theft and he would undergo a considerable torment of conscience, not because of the value of the object which might be trivial, like a pot of paint, but because the act eclipses his honesty about himself. This is a high price for the dubious pleasure of getting something for nothing. It must be said here that under universal law one cannot get anything for nothing. This is the justice of the Martial principle. One may be given something by Grace but this is a gift from on High and is not the same as that earned by merit or demerit in the psychological and physical performance of our lives. This leads on to the Jupiter principle of the soul which allows one the generosity to forgive, even oneself when there is failure or foolish forgetfulness.

From what has been said about the soul, it can be perceived that it is possible to modify the karma, or psychological reward and punishment, accrued in early life and in previous lives. The work of the emotional or moral triad, as it is called in Kabbalah, is directly concerned with dealing with such matters, so that the individual does not necessarily have to be immersed in the physical and psychological events of his fate but be as an impartial observer looking and learning from the play of his or her life. Such a viewpoint is often spoken of by various spiritual sages. As one said, 'You must see stone and gold, failure and success in much the same manner. Treat such things as phenomena of the physical and psychological worlds—to be used, but not to be attached to.' This indifference is not an uncaring one but the viewpoint of someone who has risen above his physical and psychological fate, although he might well pass through events that would cripple or destroy most people. The ability to do this is based upon not only the moment-by-moment choice to take the view of the superior person but on a vision rooted in the highest aspect of the Sun that has direct access to the World of the Spirit. This third Solar level has a cosmic outlook over events and Creation. This place in a man is where the beads of psychological choice thread themselves onto the string of free will.

19. *The Spirit*

The physical body is concerned with being in one place and time. It occupies a very small area and is restricted to a limited field of sensibility. Its duration is very ephemeral as most of it is continually decaying and being replaced, so that only a fraction of its cells are present throughout its lifespan. Indeed, what seems so solid and permanent to the physical perception is in fact quite the reverse. It is an illusion of substance, just as is the form of this book as its atoms continually vanish and are replenished by other atoms that make up the molecules and fibres of its pages. It is only the eye's relatively slow time scale that cannot perceive the sequence oscillating between something and nothing which creates the appearance of the book being present, like the static but blending frames of a movie film give the appearance of movement.

The subtle body of an individual is apparently less substantial but in fact more stable because the changes that occur in it are very gradual as compared with the carnal body's metabolism. Generally speaking, for most people there is only a little growth over a lifetime, so that they are psychologically not much older than they were at birth. The proof of this is seen in any old people's hospital ward where the essential child, so long buried beneath the acquired mask of a socially sophisticated personality, emerges again in its true immaturity. This is, in astrological terms, when the lower part of the psyche begins to lose its powers, when the lucidity and memory of Mercury and the vitality of Venus wane as the terminal stage of life is entered upon. At such a point the Moon principle within a person dims and the hidden Sun and the real level of development of the person begins to shine through. All this indicates that little conscious work has been done and that the evolution of the psychological organism has been left to the unconscious which is taught indirectly by the lessons of life that have managed to penetrate to the sleeping soul.

The soul is the receptacle of psychological Self-consciousness. It is the place where the inner alchemy of the psychological metabolism occurs. When work is done here, there are subtle changes and, like its

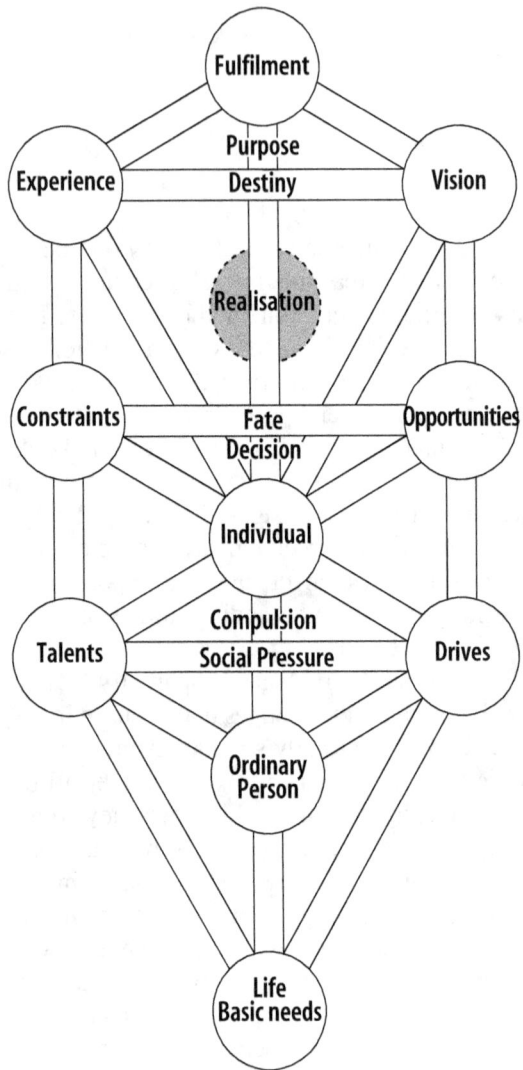

Figure 37—OPTIONS
After meeting life's basic needs and finding a place in society, one can develop one's talents and enhance one's drives so as to rise above social pressures, being a compulsive animal person to begin to become fully human. From this position one can make life-changing decisions by recognising constraints and opportunities. These can deepen the qualities of one's fate, expanding through experience and vision the realisation of what potential lies in a birth chart and actualising it in one's life. Then one's purpose and fulfilment for this incarnation is complete. (Halevi).

THE SPIRIT   171

parallel metabolic level in the body, there is a sense of ill- or well-being. However, the time scale of the soul is not limited to a daily or monthly rhythm but to the periods of the Sun, Mars and Jupiter, so that the alternation between expansion and constriction is experienced over several years, with crucial turning points occurring as these planets come into aspect with each other and the Sun that illuminates the experience for what it truly is. All this work of Martial purgatory and Jovian paradise purifies and clarifies the soul during its period of incarnation when it can, under the maximum pressure of physical existence, receive all the causes and effects of the four Worlds embodied in an incarnate person. This gives the individual a unique opportunity to perceive things he could not experience if he lived only in the upper Worlds. The operational mechanism and background of this statement, it will be remembered, is the interpenetration of the spirit into the psyche and the psyche into the body. Now, when the ascending process of evolution begins, which is counter to the creative process of descent down through the four Worlds into matter, the being starts to rise through the various levels of consciousness. First the individual becomes aware of his body or Ascendant, then the vegetable level of the Moon and then the animal level of the Sun. On attempting to become a true human being with conscience and a code of inner conduct (not to be mistaken for a conventional social morality) the soul slowly opens the door out of the physical World through the psyche into the realm of the spirit.

The realm of the spirit is the World of Creation. It is the cosmic level of existence which is vaster and less tangible but more potent than the psychological World. Indeed one might say that as the relationship of the body is to the psyche in scale, materiality and energy, so the psyche's substance and vitality is to the spirit. Perceived through analogue, it is the difference between the sea and the sky. The lower waters flow everywhere, but cling to the earth, while the upper air floats and is freer in space. Thus while the psyche takes up the form into which it is poured at birth, the spirit is beyond the confines of such earthly crystallisation. Here can be seen the function of the soul which is the intermediary between the spirit, the psyche and the body. This is accomplished through the pivot of the Sun at the centre of the psychological Tree. The point of entry into the realm of the spirit is the raising or conversion of the psychological Sun into the third or cosmic aspect of the Solar essence of an individual. Access through the spiritual Sun, as will be perceived through the kabbalistic scheme

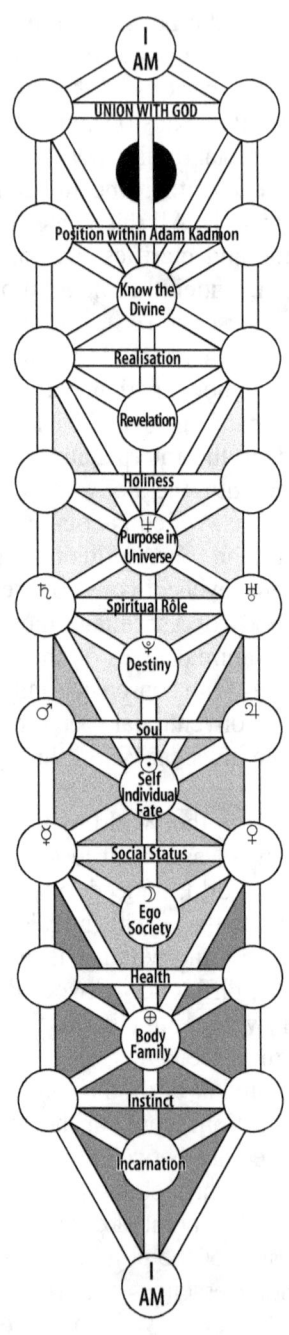

The Spirit

of the interleaved Trees of body, psyche and spirit, is into the bottommost sefirah of the World of Creation.

The World of Creation is exactly what it says. It is where everything is created, that is, brought out of Eternity and into Time where it begins to unfold its destiny and purpose. Its scale is universal and so any glimpse into this World is cosmic in flavour. There are many examples of such a vision, perhaps the most famous being the Apocalypse of St. John at the end of the New Testament where he is shown, in allegory, the End of the World. Not so generally known is the Hebrew book of Enoch in which a rabbi is shown, in a cosmic insight, all the generations of mankind and their history. The time scale of this level is immense. Take, for example, the prophets of the Old Testament who specialised in this cosmic view. Some saw the span of several hundred years to visualise the fall of Greece, Rome or Persia. However, these are relatively short distance visions compared to what Buddha and Mohammed perceived in their moments of cosmic consciousness. Moses, it is said, glimpsed the back of Eternity, which is beyond Time, but this is the World above Creation, that is the Divine.

Seen astrologically and kabbalistically, the great triad composed of Saturn, Uranus and the Sun encompasses that part of the World of the spirit and Creation within an incarnate human being. The reason for this is as follows. The Sun, as said, is the pivot of the being. It is the enlightening factor, the junction of all other planetary principles. It is mankind's link to the stars and the Milky Way which belongs to the galactic and cosmic level of Existence. Thus it is via the Sun that a person makes intimate connection with these upper Worlds and this is why the Sun is so important in a horoscope—because it contains the spiritual hub of his nature.

The planet Saturn, with its slow period, is the definer of the form of a life. It is the principle concerned with organising experience into understanding as the slow process of reason perceives, over the years, the pattern worked through the life. As a reflective principle it interprets,

---

Figure 38 (Left)—ASCENT
This Ladder sets out the path spoken of in all spiritual traditions. Astrology can be the gateway into the higher Worlds if it is seen as an esoteric discipline and not just as a mode of analysis or passive acceptance. Climbing this Ladder takes great effort but so too does any worthwhile occupation. People with easy birth charts are at a disadvantage because it makes them lazy while individuals with tough horoscopes can be spurred by the challenge. Providence designs every fate to fit the need of a person; whether they wish to take advantage is their choice. (Halevi).

in the hindsight of the Sun and lower planets, the significance of this or that event in the thirty-year periodic reappraisal of the life progression. As the outermost planet visible to the normal naked eye, it represents the largest and longest time scale wherein a physical man can comprehend something larger than his own experience. In ancient days, Saturn was not only seen as Chronos, or the god of Time, but was called the Watcher on the Threshold. This title was in recognition of the planet's guardianship of the margin between the natural and the supernatural Worlds. By this is meant that the Saturn principle in the psyche is the limit that a psychologically but not spiritually well-developed person can reach but not go beyond. There are many examples of this in history where the most learnèd of scholars and, indeed, thinkers hit a barrier which the intellect cannot cross and reason falls short. Here is where Uranus plays its part.

Uranus represents the intellectual function of revelation. It is the planet of the moment of inspiration. As the word implies, this is a drawing in of the Spirit whose Hebrew word *Ruah* also means 'Wind' or 'Air.' This, according to some Kabbalists, is the symbolic element of the World of Creation. The implication is that the Uranus principle gives access to the active rather than the reflective creative processes and so, in moments of revelation, the person sees visions of the actual workings of Creation as against the reasoned, reflective speculation of its systems when viewed by Saturn. The scale again is cosmic but also dynamic and is recognised in the flashes of genius and the enormous creative power granted to the recipient. In the unprepared, or unbalanced, this Uranian influx can be disastrous and so, before any person is allowed consciously to enter this realm, much careful training in theory and practice is undergone so as to be able to cope with any cosmic or spiritual experience that might occur, by day or night or during a Saturn or Uranus aspect of a major kind.

Situated in the centre of the spiritual triangle is the planet Pluto. This eccentrically-orbited dwarf planet is one of the most remote members of the Solar system. It represents, in this scheme, the point of transition between the Solar system and the Milky Way. As such its orbit is believed to act as a transformer for energy and substance flowing in and out of the Solar system. This same principle operates within the human psyche. While Neptune, the planet between Uranus and Pluto, is concerned with the outermost margin of the regular planetary rhythms, Pluto is not under the same set of laws and harmonies. As said, its orbit is quite unlike any of the others in that it

The Spirit

wanders occasionally inside the orbit of Neptune and has its path far out of inclination to all the other planetary planes. It has been suggested that it does not actually belong to the Solar system and, if Providence is as good a stage manager about so small an event as two people meeting as if by accident, then it is to be believed that Pluto's strange relationship to the Solar system is no accident, either, but a very precise cosmic function. All that can be said is that speculation suggests that it is a crucial link between what is in the Solar system and what lies outside. In human terms this means that Pluto brings about profound inner changes and astrological observation bears this out. Thus we have in this complex of Sun, Saturn, Uranus and Pluto, a cosmic dimension within the deep psyche, that is for most of humanity a potential possibility within the collective unconscious that operates in mundane astrology through the mind of a nation and its destiny. However, here we are considering the principle in relation to the evolving individual who makes contact with this level within himself.

When a person who has been working upon his soul reaches a certain point, he begins to perceive that his own nature, and that of others working upon their souls, is slowly building up a picture of what fate is about. It becomes more and more apparent that each life is not a random configuration but a carefully considered piece of a great jigsaw which, to the ego mind, is impossible to see. As one proverb puts it, 'How can a frog know what an ocean is?' This jigsaw is, at first, only perceived in fragments with large gaps in between. But slowly the whole general scheme is sensed, however dimly, via the reflection of Saturn, the flash of Uranus or the unmanifest transformation of Pluto that slowly alters the individual's view of the World. Bit by bit, history takes on a new meaning, and personal events new depth, as subtle connections are revealed with remote places, times and people. At first the wonder of this awakening of ancient memories is a fascination in itself and then awesome in its implication as, more and more, the evolving person sees that he has been involved over many lifetimes in a vast game, a cosmic contest in which he must either participate as an unconscious pawn or a conscious knight, bishop or even a Queen or King, as some people in history have actually had to do. This realisation brings out the question of choice; but choice of a major kind in which the real significance of free will is seen. The classic example of this was Christ's dilemma when he saw that he had a particular rôle to play in order that a new spiritual impulse might enter the Western world. While only a few are called to act out such a major historic rôle, all of us are, nevertheless, involved in some task of cosmic destiny. But before we can contemplate what that might be, we have to examine free will in the light of the endless contest between good and evil and order and chaos.

20. Evil, Free Will and the Cosmos

According to Kabbalistic tradition, evil begins with Creation. Prior to this there was only the perfect Divine and unchanging World of direct Emanation from the Godhead. But with the emergence into Existence of the World of Creation comes the first separation. This is because Creation is at one remove from Divinity in that it is a reflection of the emanated aspects of the Godhead. As such it is, to a degree, detached from the direct presence of God and therefore imperfect. Now, biblical myth declares that while the archangels and angels have remarkable powers they have no free will. This is because these inhabitants of the upper Worlds are incomplete beings. The very fact that all their names end with the syllable 'el'—like Michael, Gabriel and Haniel—indicates that they serve God's will and are under his direction. Only man, we are told, has the option of free will. Let us look at the background to this unique phenomenon.

Before man was created, biblical legend tells us, the Universe was brought into existence in a series of stages. First Heaven and Earth were created—that is, that which is above and that which is below, or the two poles of Spirit and Matter. At this point, the Bible informs us, the Earth was void and without form, that is, it was as yet an incomplete reality. Then Light was called forth, that is the will of God streaming out of the Divine World. This was then divided into day and night, or the active and passive sides of Creation, with the Divine Will as the pillar of equilibrium between. The three pillars having been set in relation to the two poles, the framework of Creation was then filled out by the firmament or macrocosm with its waters, dry land, grass, herbs, seasons and days with greater and lesser lights and stars. Then the fish of the sea and the fowl of the air, or the angels and archangels, were created and assigned to the superior and inferior parts of the upper Worlds. On the sixth day God created the beasts of the Earth, that is those creatures that were eventually to live in the lower Worlds, as yet unformed or made. God finally made Adam after God's own image, before resting on the seventh and last day of the allegory of the Creative Octave.

The creation of man at the end of the process is seen as highly significant. Firstly, it means that man contains all the other previous creations and their experience and, secondly, that man was the only complete creature, being made in the image of his Creator. This includes the Divine privilege of free will.

It is said that no other creature but man possesses this privilege. The *Elyonim* or those who dwell above are just as bound by their limits as the *Tahattonim* or those who dwell below. By this is meant that the angelic intelligences are as confined by their celestial form and energy as any animal in the natural World below. Only man can move freely about and through all the Worlds. At least that was his privilege, until the Fall. The Fall was precipitated by the encounter between free will and evil.

Evil is not a straightforward thing. There are many different kinds of evil. Firstly, there is the simple principle of separation from source and its subsequent acquired freedom of action, like a young child running away from its parent and exercising its individuality. A wise parent will allow this event but be watchful because the child, through inexperience, might come to harm. However, with increased experience the child, or creation of the parent, can sometimes refuse to come back and so go its own will-ful way. This, it is said, was the option that Lucifer, the most brilliant of the archangels, took in relation to his Creator before all the angelic hosts were brought directly under the Will of God. However, even this defection served its cosmic purpose, as we shall see later. The other lesser forms of evil are more mechanical, like the processes of decay and degeneration which are a necessary part of Creation in order to break down and clear out redundant situations. The analogue of a sewage operation illustrates the point at a cosmic level. This may appear to be a noxious and therefore evil element in the World but it is, in fact, an absolutely basic necessity, like death that releases and makes for new possibilities. The third kind of evil is that of Chaos. This, we are told by tradition, relates to the remnants of previous creations that were discarded by God as the Creator experimented with Existence. There are supposed to have been at least six models prior to our present Universe. The effect of these residual factors is that, as unattached positive and negative forces and forms, they become the demonic hosts that seek to attack and either enter and dominate Creation or steal from it and set up their own Universe. In traditional terms, they are viewed as the opposition of Chaos to the order of Creation.

Figure 39—OPPOSITION
In the course of development there is always resistance. When someone begins to climb the Ladder of Evolution, certain factors in life or within the Nature of the person will arise to oppose development. In astrology they are the negative attributes of each sign or celestial body. With Mercury's shadow side it can be disease, the very opposite to the Mercurial Healer. Venus' dark aspect is lust while that of Mars is anger and of Jupiter, profligacy. Saturn and Uranus' afflictions are rigidity and erraticism; Neptune and Pluto's are delusion and Self-destruction. The Sun and Moon's negative sides are inflation and lunacy. (Woodcut, 16th century),

Thus it was before Adam and Eve appeared in the third and subtle World of Formation, that evil already existed. With the gift of free will, and therefore temptation, such a couple and their activities were bound to be a battleground between the ordered hosts of dynamic Creation and demonic arrays of Chaos, led by the perverse intelligence of Lucifer embodied in the symbol of the serpent. While we moderns may regard these stories as quaint or even naïve, they contain the essence of the human dilemma because in the confrontation between free will and evil comes the hazard element so vital to growth and evolution.

If the Universe were totally under a Divine Will that allowed no free will, then it would be absolutely mechanical. Nothing would happen out of a pattern and nothing truly new could ever emerge or evolve. On the other hand, if the Universe were allowed totally to go its own way then it would quickly begin to degenerate and then to disintegrate. Somewhere between absolute fixed order and absolute flexibility lies the balance for an evolving but stable Existence. Here is where Adam and Eve fit into the scheme. On the one side are the forces of Order, on the other those of Chaos. Between stands mankind who can, by choice, balance the shifting fulcrum within the ebb and flow of the creative and evolutionary processes.

Like an individual's life which has good and bad periods, so the life of the Universe passes through epochs of ease or harmony and tension or disharmony. This is because the macrocosm is also growing and maturing as it moves through its cosmic cycle. There are, for example, distinct periods when the forces of Chaos are pressing hard upon Order as Creation goes through perhaps a vulnerable transition stage, just as adolescents pass through a time of confusion as they relinquish their childhood. Or there are moments in cosmic history when the balance of Order and Chaos is equal and nothing seems to happen until there is an emphasis one way or the other. Likewise, there are also periods of rapid expansion when Creation, having finished with a dissolving or barren phase, undergoes an enormous impulse of growth. These vast celestial events are, of course, reverberated down through the subtle to the physical Worlds where we perceive them, for instance, in the periods of great Earth changes like Ice Ages in the long term or, in the short, in peculiar weather conditions like prolonged drought or flood. On the human level they are seen in historical eras of economic boom and recession and the bloom and decay of high civilisations.

Seen astrologically, the planets Saturn, Uranus and Pluto, which are associated with deep space and the World of the Spirit, are considered the cosmic instruments of change. Saturn, the planet of slow, ordered progression, is the guide of gradual modification while Uranus, the planet of revelation, is the principle of sudden and revolutionary transitions. These two planets both balance and oppose one another, depending upon their mutual aspects and relation in the Zodiac. It's said, for example, that in the summer of 1976 when Saturn was in Leo, the sign of empirical despotism, and squared to Uranus in Scorpio, the sign of hidden forces, death and the legacy of the past, there came about the most remarkable change in Africa. Rhodesia, so long a white minority system of government, suddenly conceded to the principle of black majority rule, while major riots took place in South Africa where the white-dominated black population had been traditionally acquiescent. Although these events themselves may seem very local, the historical implications were global in relation to the attitude of the peoples of the world to each other as human beings. The colonial era that was several hundred years old was finally coming to an end. The imbalance generated by the dominant and subservient situation between peoples and individuals was being corrected by the pursuit of justice and human dignity. This evolutionary process, during the same period, was simultaneously at work all round the world from Russian dissidents fighting their repressive political system to the American Indians securing their rights as full US citizens. Simultaneously, extreme demonic elements took advantage of the imbalance to increase the Chaos for its own sake in unnecessary violence and guerilla outrage against Order.

Pluto, the hidden planet of deep change, is concerned directly with matters of the spirit. Its principle of unseen transformation operates beyond the rôles of Uranus and Saturn. Out of these two advocates of revolutionary force and conservative form come many combinations. Sometimes, to use our example of political change, evil uses the Saturn effect to hold back development and retard growth and so it becomes repressive. Sometimes an excessively active Uranus precipitates far too rapid a change that shocks and disrupts an order which cannot take so fast a shift and a whole society collapses, as happened in early revolutionary Russia. Pluto, as the underlying intervener that corrects and continues the transformation despite the braking action of Saturn or the accelerating function of Uranus, acts as the inherent knowledge of a nation that carries it through major traumas.

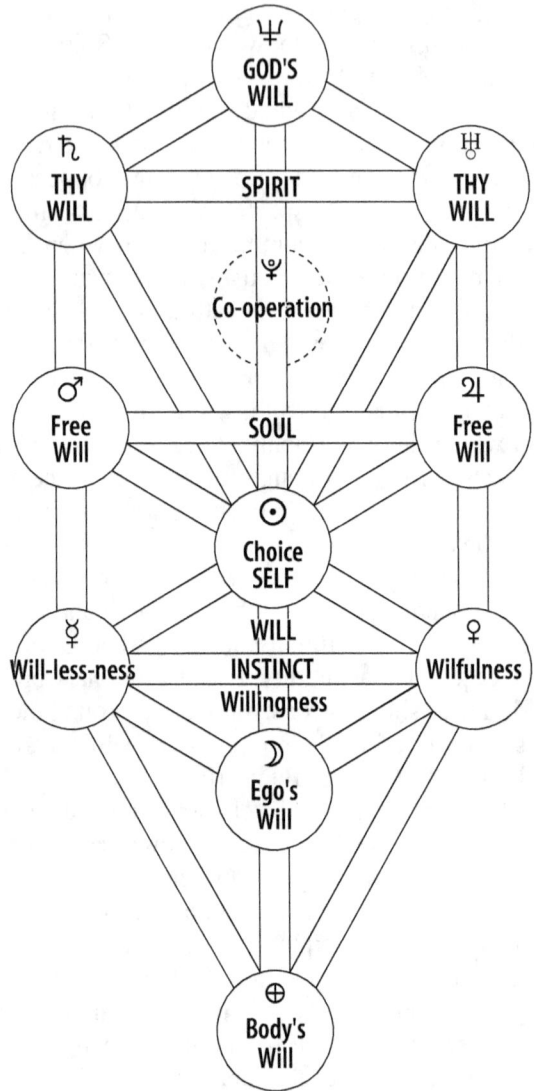

Figure 40—FREE WILL
This is a major element in personal evolution. One has to strive with the body's instincts, the ego's conditioning and the will-less-ness of the left side passive planets and the wilfulness of the active planets. In order to overcome them one has to become willing, that is, receptive, in order to acquire the animal level of will that can then be transformed into 'free will' under the control of the soul. Then it is possible to submit one's fate to the service of the universe and the Spirit and so come to co-operate with the WILL of the DIVINE. (Halevi).

On the individual scale, the Plutonian principle is the deep movement within a person that continues the progress of the spirit despite periodic advances and retreats and the long times when nothing seems to happen. It is this cosmic connection that allows the battle between good and evil to aid the onward progress of the Earth and mankind, despite the apparent resolutions and dissolutions of global conditions and human fortunes, both mass and individual.

Returning to the myth of Adam and Eve we can now begin, perhaps, to perceive the crucial rôle of conscious free will. The biblical story tells how they could do more or less what they liked. One of the things they must not do, however, was eat of the Tree of Knowledge. This placed them, as the image of their Maker, in the unique position of having choice. Now this Adam and Eve were not the Adam of the World of Creation but the divided male and female souls in the World of Formation. If one reads the first chapter of Genesis very carefully it will be observed that the process of bringing Eve into being is *formation*, not creation. The Hebrew is very explicit about this. This means that the archetypes of separated male and female principle existed in the psychological but not in the spiritual World.

The Tree of Knowledge in the midst of the Garden of Eden was the access point to the World of Creation and when they ate of it their view of Existence was profoundly changed. The exercise of free will has this quality. With the responsibility of free will, the psychological Adam and Eve then saw with the Knowledge of the Spirit. Suddenly they were no longer the innocent children of the Garden of Forms but had access to the powers of the World of Creation. This realisation led to their prompt removal by the Lord God, for the Universe's sake, down one World to be placed under the constraint of the tight laws of the physical plane and to wear clothes of flesh so that they could not reach up and so take of the Tree of Life or the Divine World and become 'one of us' or the Divine Elohim, as the text says. The gift of free will was still left with them, despite the fact that they had become, for now obvious reasons, limited in perception while living in the Natural World. The situation is still with us who are incarnate today.

The full meaning of the above biblical analogue is that while a human being may be born into this or that situation, he still contains the gift of choosing this or that for himself. This now-limited privilege, as has been many times stated, is rarely fully exercised by most people, for their first choice is *not* to use it and take on the responsibility for their own lives. Instead they opt to live under the various degrees of

Ascendant, Moon or physical Sun. Those who wish to ascend out of the confining natural laws of mass habit begin by developing first their individual will so as to be able to take on the governorship of their lives. The next step is to rise above the encapsulation of planetary fate. The planetary level of Existence is parallel to the mythical Garden of Eden where the job of Adam and Eve is that of being the gardeners of that subtle World. As such they, and any human being who reached this psychological level, can enjoy the pleasures of Paradise or the pains of Purgatory according to the performance of the individual. However, with Adam and Eve's taste of Knowledge, now absorbed into the human being, the involvement in the World of Creation cannot be denied and so it is possible for a spiritually developed person to rise above his fate and enter the World of Creation and so participate in the cosmic drama and consciously assist in the great battle between Order and Chaos. This exercise of free will can, via the principle of a person's inner Pluto or the dark mirror of visionary consciousness, lead to the perception of the vast and deep panorama of the cosmic situation. Often this level of comprehension is dramatically played out in significant inner and outer events of an individual's fate, where the confrontation between good and evil is presented in symbolic and actual terms—like Christ's forty days in the wilderness with Satan. For it is a man's option to work for either side of the cosmic game.

Kabbalistic tradition says that everything we do contributes to one side or the other of the celestial battle; that the human race alone has the ability to influence the cosmic balance from below. Thus a person can, because of an act of free will, individually affect the efforts of the angels and demons. Now, as we have seen, this can only be generally said of those people who are striving to be true individuals, because those who live off either Ascendant, Moon or physical Sun are, for the most part, unconsciously moved about by the ebb and flow of celestial tides, like seaweed and seashore creatures. However, even they, in their periodic moments of psychological and spiritual awakening, can affect the battle, as has sometimes actually been the case by an act of individual physical or moral bravery or sacrifice by someone who normally would never have stepped outside the habitual pattern of a situation. Joan of Arc and William Tell were such people. For the person who is consciously attempting to view the world from the position of the cosmic standpoint, the situation usually means acting against what the ordinary world at large thinks and does. Such people often have to perform, in relation to events in the unseen upper Worlds, strange historic enactments on Earth in order to bring about a change that will have a profound long-term effect in the lower Worlds, perhaps centuries later. Moses and Christ are examples of this. Thus it is that everyone who wishes to can begin to fulfil his destiny by taking up, to a greater or lesser degree, the opportunity to affect the balance of cosmic Order and Chaos and further the evolution of the Universe.

These opportunities are provided in everyone's life by Heaven or the World of Creation which designs into every fate the already mentioned moments of physical, psychological and spiritual crisis so that no one is deprived of their chance to participate. This operation of Providence we will now examine in detail.

21. Providence

Providence originates at the level of the cosmic World of Creation. It is the providing of what is necessary at a certain time and place when it is needed. There are two main reasons why this is possible. The first is that this spiritual level has the power to create conditions in the Worlds below and the second is that it is this World that is in charge of Time.

It will be recalled that the World of Divine Emanation is Time-full and perfect, that is, everything to be brought into existence is unmanifest yet complete because it exists in Eternity. However, it is not until the creative process begins that the potential begins to become actual. In the World of Creation this manifests in the movement out of the Eternal Unchanging into the unfolding of the destiny of a thing, be it an archangel, galaxy, star, stone or a man. Here the thing called forth by the Divine begins its descent to that World where it will fulfil its purpose. Some things or beings will only descend to one World, others to two and yet others to three to exist in the realm of physical action and elements. Thus we see a creative sequence extending out of the World of Emanation first to create and form a cosmos which is then slowly inhabited by beings, some of whom live exclusively in the upper and some exclusively in the lower Worlds, with mankind hovering between. This sequence has a time order and no event happens before its preparation has been completed and its result calculated to affect other events to follow in the grand design. This is the essence of Time.

The general plan of Creation, we are told, has been worked out. Its design was conceived so that the Will of God shall be fulfilled. However, while the broad flow of time and events is set the details, especially as regards mankind, are not. Firstly the unfolding of the sequences has, as said, crucial moments when the progression is either moving very slowly or when it is unfolding very quickly. These periods are moments when the general equilibrium is off balance and therefore subject to successful assault by the forces of Chaos. Such epochs are, however, vital because they are usually associated with

Figure 41 — PROVIDENCE
This image shows the two sides of fate. On the left the blindfolded lady symbolises allowing oneself to be totally at the mercy of general circumstances and cosmic weather. On the right, the lady can see the ever-changing celestial configuration and adjust accordingly. A kabbalistic astrologer takes into account when to act and when not to take action as regards their fate and the worldly situation. Knowledge is power; in this case, how to avoid disaster or take full advantage of even difficult transits or trends. One must trust Providence but respond intelligently to all the omens sent as guidance. (Medieval woodcut).

critical turning points or changes that cannot occur during the constant velocity periods. It is rather like changing the quality of a human relationship. During the ordinary periods not much happens but, when things become either very slow or too fast, things that cannot be said or happen in the periods of straight running can be said or done. This is one of the functions of crisis. So it is with Creation and Time where everything has its season and crisis points. The general work of Providence is to provide the balancing and offsetting factors which correct or change the mechanical course of events that tend to run down or run up to an off-balanced state if left to themselves. Tradition has it that there is a band of archangelic intelligences who oversee such matters. They are called, in Hebrew, the *Irin*, the *Gregori* in Greek or the Watchers in English. Their task is to supervise events and make sure nothing malfunctions in Creation because, it will be recalled, imperfection or evil begins with the creative process and quite minor faults at this cosmic level can be multiplied into major disasters in the Worlds below.

Now again while the general cosmic plan is unfolding to create, form and make physical galaxies, suns, planets and Nature, the details are left open. However, these details are confined by the laws of the lower Worlds to a certain number of options which are expressed in the variation in the stars, planets and natural forms. However, while these natural forms, for example, have a wide variety they are all nevertheless rooted in a basic pattern of their species. For instance, there are many kinds of bird but all birds are founded upon the same model with each species, despite its size and proportions, always conforming to the archetypal bird skeleton and organs. It is the same with stars that follow the universal template of atomic process, although they may be of very different size, stage and composition. This freedom of detail is designed to allow for flexibility in responding to the fluctuations of the grand design of the Universe as it moves through the travail of Creation and Evolution—in the case of mankind the limits are infinitely wider and for quite a different reason.

Mankind is, we are instructed, unique in that it has the capability of ranging throughout the three lower Worlds of physical, psychological and spiritual experience. Moreover the human race, wherever it may be in the Universe (and there is good reason to believe we are not the only human beings in the cosmos) has the option of aiding or inhibiting Creation. This means, to a greater or lesser degree, that an individual can influence his own and the general situation. However, as we have seen, only a fraction of the human race has developed this capacity fully and most people are held by their own choice within the general law of large masses or that individual's fate. This, as said, does not preclude choice at certain points that can transform a life from a purely physical existence or a fatal pattern into something approaching true free will. Such a possibility means that there are two levels of Providence as regards human beings.

The first task of Providence is to provide a suitable environment for the incarnate soul. This is usually done without difficulty as millions are born each year into homes where, for the most part, they are provided for by caring parents. Moreover, Providence creates an unfolding situation that is exactly what the person needs, although not always what he may think he wants or desires. This general pattern can be applied to those who live under their Ascendant or Moon. Providence also makes sure that, at certain crucial points, the right circumstance provides a spouse or a job or house when needed, often against apparently hostile odds. This is called luck by those who are unaware of the workings of higher Worlds. Providence also creates very difficult circumstances to reveal or dissolve a fixed situation like a dead marriage or an unhealthy occupation. This is called bad luck or later, 'a blessing in disguise.' The reason for this is that evil ultimately comes from God and is therefore concerned with the development of the individual. Everyone has experienced these phenomena. They are inexplicable in physical logic, just as are fatal meetings that bring people, born thousands of miles apart, together and keep people born in the next block away from each other for years until they are ready to meet.

As will be realised, fate is simply the fine focus of Providence. Whereas people under the Ascendant and Moon can only be aided at critical times when they are relatively awake psychologically or spiritually, people with some individuality are more sensitive to subtle conditions and so are more directly in contact with the fluctuations of cosmic events. Because of this they meet Providence half-way and life seems to follow that distinct sequence known to us as a remarkable fate. Now fate, as we have seen, is set out in the natal chart in as much as the tendencies shown are acted upon by the movements and developments of the upper Worlds and the conscious or unconscious response of the individual. This pattern has, in fact, been selected by Providence to be of mutual service to Creation and that individual, because both need each other in order to fulfil the grand design.

However, there is choice and so the full potential of a human life can be ignored by the person burying himself in the physical World. In contrast, fate can be lived out to the full in the subtle World in preparation to be able to live in the spiritual realm. Now here Providence shows its power, for while it will take care of the natural man in a general way and guide the fate of a psychologically developed person through their lives, it will actually change or create new situations for a spiritually-oriented individual. This is called the miraculous.

Before we define what a miracle is, let us at least sense this level through an astrological principle. Neptune is considered to be concerned with matters of Providence. It is traditionally regarded as a puzzling planet, vague in its effect. Situated at the most remote point in the Solar system (because Pluto is not considered to be a true member of the planetary organisation) it is the orbit or sphere that connects things beyond with things within. Likewise its position on the sefirotic Tree is at the Crown at the top and here it is also the connection with what is beyond. In astrology it is the planet most concerned with setting the mood of a time as its orbit takes over a decade to pass through each sign. Its effect is related to 'things mysterious' and we can see, by its position on the extended Ladder of the four Worlds, that its principle occupies the place where it is in simultaneous contact with the subtle, spiritual and Divine Worlds. This gives it direct access to the Will of the Divine, the centre of Creation and the Crown of the psychological World which means that the power of Divine or Providential intervention is possible via the Neptunian principle. Seen in an historical example, Neptune's quality is well demonstrated by the period during which it was in the sign of hidden things, Scorpio, from 1956 to 1971. This was the epoch when the interest in matters of the unseen, ranging through the drug scene, magic and meditation to oriental religion, became a normal and accepted interest in the West. In the individual chart it represents that hidden and spiritual connection, when well-aspected, or the blurred and confused element in the psyche, if afflicted. In all cases great and small it is the factor associated with the most rarefied, odd, strange, wondrous and miraculous.

The definition of a miracle is when a superior World intervenes in an inferior World. Generally speaking this does not occur. It is not necessary because, for the most part, Creation runs along pretty predictable lines, patterns and rhythms. However, there are occasionally times when an emergency arises because someone with some free will has made a mistake (and it does happen) and unleashed certain forces that have to be contained or cancelled. On the positive side it happens when something miraculous needs to be demonstrated to indicate that there are other Worlds or someone with a special spiritual task needs help. Of the first and negative case there would be very little recorded because such a situation is never allowed to develop beyond its initial stage.

For example, someone with evil intent might be made simply to forget a trigger element in an explosive situation or miss a crucial meeting, be removed or die naturally but unexpectedly, which defuses a circumstance which could have had wide repercussions. This has occurred many times in history and in spiritual work where a man chose to use power for his own ends. The second case of demonstration of higher levels of reality is well illustrated by many Bible stories, ranging from the ten plagues to Christ's miracles. All were to point out that the law of the lower Worlds was not absolute but that it could be overruled by supernatural interests. A minor instance of Providence or a local miracle is not at all uncommon to anybody on the spiritual path when, for example, a certain book which is supposed to be unobtainable turns up exactly when needed, often freely given by someone who has no use for it. A more dramatic example is when perhaps a person is prevented from flying on a certain plane that later crashes. There are many instances of this phenomenon. Now, while they can be taken as coincidence, the very fact that they coincide, especially in their often meticulous timing, is highly indicative of a remarkable level of stage management. Indeed, the characteristic of such providential incidents is that while the odd event may seem, on the surface, casual or accidental, the long-term result of it never is and always fits into a concern that is to do both with that person's spiritual development and their contribution to the grand design of Creation.

What does this mean astrologically? The significance is that the pattern of fate is designed as a prelude to a life of the spirit. This means that fate is a preparation, a testing and a training programme for each person, to find out what he can and cannot do and what his individual task is before he is given the power and responsibility to participate in the drama of Creation. All this, however, does not mean that a person avoids the fate set for him but that he perceives his life's pattern from a spiritual and cosmic dimension.

Let us take, for an example of the above, a man with Sun in Pisces in the 12th House. This would indicate a very withdrawn person, intensely shy or, if negatively aspected, prone to almost compulsive retirement into a private world of dreams. Depending upon the rest of the chart and its aspects, one would expect to find such a person working at home, in an institution or even in prison. If the person had, say, Jupiter conjunct the Sun he might even be a monk. All these, as will be seen, indicate a deep desire for seclusion, be it externally imposed by the law or health or self-sought in the pursuit of privacy in work or worship. In every case the interior life would be very strong. For the prisoner, the confines of the cell would justify a fantasy of self-pity and anger. For the man working at home or in an institution, it would allow space for private speculation and interior exploration while being hidden in his room or behind the formal rôle as an official. For the monk it might be the pleasure or pain of being alone with God. Now let us assume that any one of these Pisceans undergoes a spiritual transformation. The prisoner might, and it has occasionally happened, experience a conversion in a deep state of remorse for what he has done. Or he might arrive at the same spiritual stage because, in the silence of his cell, the anger and self-pity could suddenly or gradually be seen as useless in the light of the reality of his situation. Then his cell might slowly or abruptly change from a confining tomb into a walled haven where he converses with a level of reality that has widened far beyond the physical space that imprisons his body. From that point on things would begin to change for the man. Moreover, unusual and providential things would begin to happen further to release the man. It could take the form of a change in law, a review of his case or a recognition of his altered state. It might be that he would accept prison life but show by his inner release and by personal example that a man can live with dignity and faith under such conditions. This could profoundly affect both prisoners and warders. Such cases are not unknown.

As to the other Piscean fates, the similar could occur and, although each life was deeply affected outwardly, it would remain almost the same to unperceptive eyes. The chief difference would be in the profound quality of the person and their effect on others. And here we see the way Providence works through the individual to implement the Divine Will; for the position in life, whether it be in a prison, at home, in an institution or a monastery would be exactly where such a person would be needed to lift the situation. The person working at home, for example, might be a writer or designer whose work would influence those who read and looked at it; or the official could well be the man who modified the rules of a college or introduced a wider viewpoint than the orthodox into a hospital; or the monk could be the one individual who actually experiences what the Holy Order set out to do but few of its monks had ever accomplished. Such a person could lift the monastery's life above the outwardly pious routine into a ritual with deep spiritual content.

The operation of Providence works from the general to the individual level. It begins in Creation as the manifestation of a cosmic principle, passes into form in the subtle World and is manifest in a particular event in the physical World. With a human being whose spirit was conceived in Creation the same sequence applies, except it is the form of the fate as expressed through the physical life that carries out its cosmic purpose. Each particular human fate is one of many that slots into a sequence of reincarnations, each one of which is relevant to that individual's spiritual growth and its long-term cosmic rôle. So it is that all the previous lives up till the present incarnation are related to a distinct progression called destiny which is, in turn, related to the general history of Creation. In us, it is the performance of the current life, be it in the emphasis of the body, soul or spirit, that will affect— to a greater or lesser degree—the general state of the Universe. The significance of this to the astrologer is that what lessons have been learned, what debts and credits incurred, will have had a considerable influence upon the present and future natal charts. This brings us to the always providential circumstance of death which dissolves the mould of the horoscope and releases the individual to compare his natal potential to the actual life lived in the post-mortem review as the soul unwinds its lived-out fate in hindsight.

22. Death and Destiny

Creation begins Time by emerging from the unchanging Eternal. It flows out in a great cosmic cycle called a *shemittah* in Kabbalah or a *kalpa* in Hindu esotericism. This cycle reaches its maximum extension in the physical World and then begins to return to its source where it resolves its motion in the rest and equilibrium of the Eternal Unchanging again. This cyclic pattern is repeated in diminishing degrees throughout the lower Worlds as the things and beings created pass through their birth, life and death. So it is with an individual and his life on Earth.

Death is regarded by most people as something sinister and to be feared. They witness death in nature every day and take it for granted and yet they find their own death unacceptable. This is because they cannot, or rather do not want, to look beyond the physical limitations they set upon themselves and so death becomes an unknown; thus, being ignorant of its purpose, its true nature is not perceived beyond that it destroys the body and the ego's sense of its identity. This is clearly a very distorted view which is not helped by the numerous superstitions about the phenomena associated with death.

The first thing is to recognise that death is the terminal stage of a cosmic process. All events have points of conception, birth, growth, zenith, decay and death. Death is the moment when the consciousness embodied in the flesh is lifted out of its biological confines and into an upper World. Seen in biblical terms, it is the Day of Rest at the end of the seven ages of human experience.

Seen as an act of cosmic mercy, death is the device which helps in the unexpected—an intolerable situation to be broken, an insoluble crisis to be solved—and releases, in the expected, the physically exhausted from the pain of illness or the weariness of old age. Death allows things that are stuck in a jam to be freed and mistakes that have been made to be rectified in another chance, in another life. This raises the issue of death at different periods of life, in childhood and youth, as well as in one's prime or middle age. Here we must see that different lives or fates have different purposes, both for the individual concerned and those around them.

It is said that the moment of death, like the moment of birth, is fixed and that it can be detected in the horoscope. This, as a general principle, is true; but firstly, there are few astrologers who can do this because it requires the most fastidious skill to take into account all the factors and secondly, the death indicated is not always a physical one. Let us take the astrological principles to begin with. According to astrological tradition there are factors in the horoscope that are called the 'givers' and the 'takers' of life. The Hyleg, or health and general vitality, is related, as might be expected, to the Ascendant, Moon and Sun, their disposition to one another and the aspects that they receive from the planets and positions in the Houses. The traditional Anaretas or 'takers' of life are Mars and Saturn with Uranus but the Sun may also be a factor in death. The combinations that will, theoretically, produce death are very complex and dependent upon dozens of factors like the general vitality, inclination to seek danger or be accident-prone. There are, of course, often clear indications of a type of death. For example, Uranus in the 8th House indicates a sudden end while Saturn there suggests a long-drawn-out one. These and other combinations are subject to modification by individual development or Divine intervention and so it is not advisable to predict a definite date of death. Nevertheless, there is a fatal moment of death.

There is an ancient story that a man had a servant whom he sent into the market place on an errand. When the servant returned he was very agitated. When asked why, he replied that he had seen the Angel of Death among the crowds and that it had regarded him with surprise. 'Let me take a horse and ride to the city of Samara,' begged the servant, 'so that I may escape Death.' The master agreed to the servant's request. Later that day the master went to the market and was approached by the angel who said 'Why is your servant here?' The master replied that the servant was no longer with him but had taken a fast horse to Samara. Death nodded in understanding and said, 'I was surprised to see him here because tonight I have a fatal appointment with him in Samara.'

The story illustrates well a moment of fate. Even so, death is not quite as simple as that. It can be said that the date is provisionally set in the chart but, as we know now, there is the factor of free will. Thus while the clock of life is fixed to stop at a certain point a person, by foolish choice, can shorten the time allotted to him. An example of this is the person who yields to his weakness of drink or his tendency to find exciting but dangerous situations. Thus a man of violence will

Figure 42 — DEATH
Because most people do not develop their full capacity, they die when planetary pressure and the current life karma culminate in a breaking point. A drunk's death is an extreme and inevitable example. However, an evolving individual can extend his life span by avoiding the stresses and situations many people tolerate because they see no way out. The wise, however, know how and when to leave a destructive situation. A million people die every day and just over a million are reborn to learn their lessons. (The Spiral of Discarnate Souls, Doré's illustration for Dante's *Divine Comedy,* 19th century).

perhaps become a soldier or a gangster where the likelihood of him stopping a bullet is higher than the man who sells newspapers on the same corner for fifty years of undramatic life. In a moment of deep spiritual free will, like Socrates' choice to stay in Athens and be executed, or a moment of weakness, such as a suicide, a person might choose to take his own life and thus cut the provisionally allotted lifespan short. Alternatively it is possible to defer the moment of death, either by a sustained act of will, like giving up the desire to smoke, or by glimpsing into the future and so avoid, say, a disastrous train accident that affects others.

The possibility of seeing beyond the present is not theoretically or practically impossible, as much evidence shows. This is because if Existence is seen as a vast plan, then it should be possible to project what will happen based upon the past and the present. This is what economists and weather forecasters do. In astrology the same theory applies, except there are certain advantages in that one can see the celestial situations unfold with greater and more predictable detail in relation to the mundane and personal charts. This kind of prediction, however, as must be repeated again, is contingent not only upon the consideration of every aspect, which few astrologers can manage, but upon the level of development of the individual involved. In the case of the Ascendant- and Moon-ruled person the matter is mechanical, so that the moment of death is more or less at the preset time when the malefics are bringing to bear the maximum tension on the chart's major health weakness from or in the House of death. An example of this clockwork-like type of life is seen in George III of England and an ironmonger called Hennings who were born in the same town at the identical time. They married on the same day, inherited their respective fathers' jobs in the same year, had the same number of children, suffered the same illnesses and died in the same hour. This phenomenon, called astrological twinning, only applies when both people do nothing about their psychological or spiritual growth but simply live life mechanically. In the case of the person who exercises choice, changes can be made according to the degree and depth of choice. Thus, while the basic pattern is set by the chart and events on the whole will unfold as predicted, a real change of attitude and inner state can make the difference between life or death. This leads back to the ability to foresee events.

Besides the reasoned prediction of the astrologer, there is the phenomenon of visions of the future. These may come not only in dreams but during conscious and unconscious moments that may forewarn of approaching crisis. As will have been perceived, all happenings are generated in the upper Worlds, the lesser fitting into the greater and so on down until they manifest at some point in the moment *Now* in the physical World. If the sensitivity of a person is sufficient, or the consciousness is raised above the normal level of ego and beyond the Self, it is possible to perceive an impression or intimation of oncoming tendencies that are already focusing in the subtle World. It is rather like hearing a car's engine before it rounds a bend. From this signal can be imagined the size and type of the car and so it is with oncoming events. Sometimes, depending on how good the signal is, a very precise picture can be seen and, sometimes in error, more can be read into the vision than is actually there. This is a common enough mistake among economic and political pundits with more concrete data to go on than clairvoyance. Nevertheless, the principle and the practice of prediction exists. From such a glimpse of prophecy or hint of warning evasive action can be taken and this can be seen either as an act of Providence or, indeed, part of the fatal pattern. Neptune in the 8th and 12th Houses would grant the clairvoyant faculty to be used by that individual for themselves and others. Either way a moment of possible death can be averted and so there is always the option of shortening or extending life. But let us return to the subject of death.

Seen kabbalistically, death is the separation of the physical Tree from the psychological and spiritual Trees. This disconnection brings about the immediate cessation of all organic processes and the rapid but not instant decay of the etheric body that joined the body to the psyche. The strictly physical viewpoint either does not perceive the immediate post-death processes or dismisses it as imagination. The seeing and hearing of the dead is, indeed, in imagination but this is precisely what it is for, in order to perceive the non-physical Worlds. By this same process, poets and painters work and visionaries see. Whether the phenomenon is objective or not is dependent upon the objectivity or subjectivity of the viewer, not the phenomenon. Certainly a person who only believes in physical criteria cannot be considered objective but only prepared to view things through a very narrow spectrum.

According to those who have experienced and observed death on the widest scale, the following broad series of events occurs. Such accounts are found all over the world, ranging from the *Book of the*

Zohar of Kabbalah to the Tibetan *Book of the Dead*. We will view it from an astrological standpoint.

We are told that at the moment of death the combination of planets is as relevant as those present at our birth. This suggests that, as we are projected out of the physical and into the subtle World, so the synthesis of our lives is for that moment presented to us. Indeed, traditional literature describes, in many symbolic ways, how the life just lived is reviewed in a rapid sequence like a film being unrolled. Because of its rapidity, the dead person experiences an initial assessment of all the sorrows and joys of the now-past life in a concentrated state of extreme pleasure and pain. During this period of post-mortem awareness there is, we are instructed, a possibility of freeing ourselves also from the subtle World and passing straight into the spiritual, and even beyond, but most people cling to the known with its rewards and punishment. These credits and debits are the results of the life just lived and the residue of previous lives which have accrued over many generations or incarnations. The next stage, we are informed, is one of a longer review and assessment of the life just past. This may mean periods of deep remorse or great pleasure and give rise to the myths of Purgatory and Paradise which are psychological locations and on this side and that side of death. This epoch is followed by events which are decided according to the choice of the individual. Some, for example, seek a rapid return to the physical World so desperately that they are almost instantly conceived in an incarnate couple's sexual union. These souls are thus reborn without much memory of the subtle World. Some more mature souls want a time to reflect before this occurs to learn, without the confinement of physical laws, the lessons of the last life. There are those, however, who are not reborn and they, we are told, enter the World of the Spirit to operate from the level of the wise ones of mankind, who, it is said, do occasionally descend to incarnate upon the Earth in order to carry out some cosmic assignment. The great spiritual teachers of the human race belong to this class.

For the mass of mankind the situation is a continual birth, life and death cycle with little memory of their sojourn in the subtle World. Seeking only physical comfort and satisfaction, any memory of their pre-natal state is soon forgotten and they live life after life slowly ascending, with occasional descents for misdemeanors, up the general evolutionary ladder of Existence. For people who have developed at least some Self-conscious individuality, each life contains in its fate particular strengths and weaknesses. Thus musical gifts or skill in business, as well as bad traits, are revealed in the birth charts. Indeed, also clearly shown are all the lessons to be learned and the rough times when fate will provide moments of trial. These will draw the person on to better performance and perfection or wilful ignorance and its consequence if they take the evil option. The laws that govern the Universe will demonstrate, by inevitable reaction, that they cannot be contravened. However, before the next life can begin, certain factors have to be brought together. This is the task of Providence which co-ordinates all events, both great and small, in the lower Worlds.

One factor is that all the people fatally associated with the person have to be in the right places above and below before the individual is born. This is because the group of spirits that were created to do a particular cosmic task are born always within two or three generations of each other so that they may meet and be reconnected in the physical World. When they are all relatively ready in their positions in the subtle and physical Worlds, the particular soul can then begin to re-descend for the next phase of personal and mutual development and work. The timing of these reincarnations is obviously crucial as it has to await certain conditions that are absolutely right for that group's task, as well as for the role of the individual lives. Thus we will get people who, for example, live through major wars but are either too young or too old to fight in them or are born just in time to be involved in a particular spiritual movement or political crisis, like being the man of the hour with just the right maturity and talents needed. As Churchill observed, when he was given the premiership of wartime Britain at sixty-six, this was the moment of destiny he had been unconsciously waiting for all his life.

The result of the foregoing is that people who have never met on Earth before, having been born, sometimes, thousands of miles away and with many years between them, sometimes recognise each other as being already familiar. This phenomenon has several explanations

Figure 43 (Right)—EVOLUTION
Here is the hierarchy of humanity. At the bottom are the 'living dead', that is, those who have lost, for this life, any possibility of growth. Above come the young souls who comprise the masses. Over them are their leaders. Then come those who have individuated. Beyond them come the most advanced members of incarnate humanity, at the head of which is the current Messiah who lives somewhere on Earth. Over him or her is the Great Holy Council, that is, those who no longer have to incarnate. Above them all is Enoch, alias Metatron, the first fully realised human being. (Halevi).

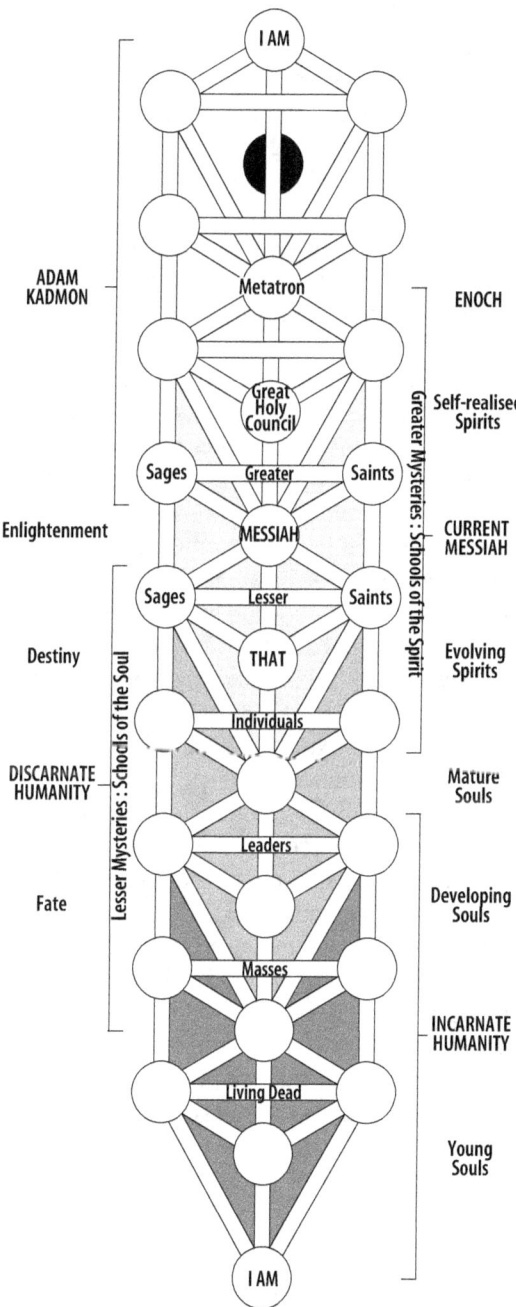

but experience shows that it often results in a fatal meeting that can end in intimate love for one, friendship for another and even enmity for yet another as a karmic drama is played out to resolve a recurring problem. In rare cases such a meeting might well be to fulfil a destiny at the cosmic level, like the young Plato's meeting with Socrates and its subsequent effect on Western and Islamic religion and philosophy.

Destiny is the purpose of each life. But taken from the view of reincarnation, it is the aim or destination of a series of lives. Each fate represents the gradual evolution of the individual as it passes down from the World of pure but naïve spirits, through the experiences of the subtle and physical Worlds to return as a matured being to the place from whence it came. Seen in traditional kabbalistic terms, the spirit within a human being is the cosmic dimension. As such it contains the Divine spark of Adam Kadmon. Together they are within each human soul which is, in turn, a cell of humanity, part of which is incarnate. These cells form organs or soul groups through which both the individual and Adam Kadmon can become Self-realised.

The process of becoming increasingly conscious is gradual. It has taken many millions of years for the Universe's consciousness to rise from the atomic into the mineral state and then into the vegetable and animal levels of awareness. Man, the most sophisticated of incarnate creatures, has covered the ascent at a steadily increasing rate as more and more spirits descend to experience the subtle and physical Worlds. The reason for this acceleration is that the physical World contains within it all the other Worlds and, although the conditions are the most tough, they are by far the most conducive for rapid growth. That is why mankind is incarnated. Thus in every incarnation of a human being there is the maximum opportunity to experience many kinds of pleasure and pain, success and failure, temptation and triumph so as to expand, deepen and strengthen its spiritual, psychological and physical being. This experiencing is accomplished not only by a number of rebirths but, we are told, by the spirit reincarnating progressively through each zodiacal sign. This can occur because the Sun, having the three levels within itself, can manifest the spirit in each psychological and physical type and so grant the individual, in his or her journey round the twelve biblical tribes or signs of the Zodiac, experience of all twelve basic viewpoints of mankind.

Thus, for example, a spirit will be born under a particular sign and live that life in the way of that sign's cosmic function. In this way the individual realises, in the various zodiacal gifts and difficulties, a destiny that underlies the series of fates through which the spirit passes. Each human spirit, moreover, will be accompanied through the various incarnations by other human spirits, some of which will be spiritually older and some spiritually younger, some imparting to it instructions and some to which it imparts aid to help their fulfilment. It will form during its many lifetimes certain relationships, some which will be close and some distant, that will bring out the best and worst of its nature and thus test and develop its capacity in preparation to perform its cosmic work. During the first incarnations it will be confused but later, as it achieves the level of the soul, it will begin to know and recognise its place, first among its friends and foes and then its rôle among its gradually recognised spiritual companions. The chain of many fates, when fused, becomes the conscious destiny of that individual. That is, to become an image of God in miniature.

The destiny of each individual and the purpose of mankind is to reflect, in consciousness, the macrocosm to its Maker. Since mankind has been on Earth, more and more spirits have descended to the Natural World who, after their sojourn here, rise and occupy the subtle World of Paradise or live in the spiritual World of Heaven according to their accomplishment. Thus all the three lower Worlds are inhabited not only by those who only dwell below, like the beasts of the field, and those who only dwell above, as the angels do, but by those who can consciously exist in the physical, psychological and spiritual Worlds. This is called, in Kabbalah, the Unification of the Worlds or the purpose of mankind. In this way Adam, the image of the Divine, fulfils God's will to behold God, until the End of Time when the mirror of Existence dissolves into union with the One that was, is and will always be and be not.

ADONAI EHAD

www.ingramcontent.com/pod-product-compliance
Lightning Source LLC
Chambersburg PA
CBHW072051110526
44590CB00018B/3129